D0034197

# Tame Your Inner Critic

© Daniel Hirsh

## About the Author

Della Temple has a bachelor's degree in business administration/accounting and a master's degree in organizational leadership (string theory for business nerds). She combines her love of anything analytical with her wide-ranging interest in quantum physics and the world of energetic healing. She is a certified Reiki Master and has studied clairvoyance and psychic healing at Boulder Psychic Institute, working under the direction of Miwa Mack.

Della believes that being psychic is a very natural state of being. It is a skill, just like playing the piano or singing on key. It takes a teacher, a willingness on the part of the student to be receptive to new ideas, and some time spent in practice. In her book *Tame Your Inner Critic,* Della invites readers to experience opening to their own intuition on the journey toward discovering their life's purpose. She is currently writing her second book, *Conscious Grieving: Spiritual Tools to Help You Navigate the Loss of a Loved One,* about her experiences after her son Rick's death four years ago.

Della lives with her husband in the mountains above Boulder, Colorado, and visits the island of Maui every winter. Contact her at della@dellatemple.com, visit her website at www.dellatemple.com, or follow her at DellaTempleAuthor on Facebook.

DELLA TEMPLE

# Tame Your Inner Critic

Find Peace & Contentment
to Live Your Life
on Purpose

Llewellyn Publications
Woodbury, Minnesota

First Edition
First Printing, 2015

Cover art: Thinkstock/482044511/©amovitania
Cover design by Lisa Novak
Interior art by Mary Ann Zapalac

Llewellyn Publications is a registered trademark of Llewellyn Worldwide Ltd.

"Attitudes" copyright © 1981, 1982 by Charles R. Swindoll, Inc. All rights are
    reserved worldwide. Used by permission.

**Library of Congress Cataloging-in-Publication Data (Pending)**
ISBN: 978-0-7387-4395-0

Llewellyn Publications
A Division of Llewellyn Worldwide, Ltd.
2143 Wooddale Drive
Woodbury, MN 55125-2989
www.llewellyn.com

Printed in the United States of America

*To Rachel,*
*Spirit Friend and writing partner*

## Acknowledgments

First, foremost, and always: To my husband and companion, David. Without your support, I wouldn't have taken the first steps down the path of becoming more. From the very beginning you saw the shining star of my soul, encouraging me to walk this unknown path. When I was unsure and my inner critic started to take over, you were there to remind me of who I truly am.

To my reading fairies, a group of dedicated clairvoyants with whom I've traveled this path of enlightenment: Cristyn Cairns, Tarin Davies, Meave Foley, Katherine Ganev, Heidi Green, Lisa Klare, Sara Pearl, Mary Riker, Nancy Trottner, and Lisa Witter. Your technical comments and neutral yet passionate endorsement gave me the courage to get this to print.

To my editing elves: Caroline Garhart, who took a very rough draft and gave it structure, to Beth and Jody who carried it a little bit further down the path, and to Laurel Kallenbach (laurelkallenbach.com), whose gentle prodding allowed me to stand in my own power and claim my place as an author.

To my Spirit Friends: I am full of gratitude for your guidance and encouragement. For opening closed doors, shining up dull manuscripts so they were seen by editors, and opening the doors wide so I could walk my path. I am so full of gratitude and in awe of this world of energy.

To Miwa Mack, a very wise psychic and excellent teacher. I am blessed to have learned under your tutelage. Your classes are always full of love, laughter, encouragement, and ease. Blessings!

# Contents

# Figures

# Exercises

# Introduction

My inner critic used to be very loud and obnoxious. It told me I couldn't do many of the things I really wanted to do, that I was too small, too unprepared, too opinionated, or just not good enough. This voice told me that I needed to change, that I wasn't good enough just as I was. I presented a great face to the world, yet deep within I was struggling with issues of self-worth and self-criticism. I had grown so used to the incessant negativity that I really believed I was deficient in some way.

Sound familiar?

If your inner critic is as unbearable as mine used to be, then I have a message for you: I have tamed my inner critic and you can too. I have found the peace and contentment I craved. I know I'm fine just the way I am—no, I'm better than I ever expected to be! I listen to a new voice now, one that fills me with love, compassion, and gentleness. I am comfortable in my own skin, liking all parts of me, even those not-so-perfect parts. As a result, the relationship I have with myself and with others has blossomed. This voice is Spirit, my true essence, talking directly to me. By listening to this new voice, I am now expressing my unique life purpose and living the life I was meant to live.

This book is designed to help you tame the loud, persistent chatter of your inner critic and replace it with the voice of your inner guidance, your Spirit. As you do so, your inner world will become a place of stillness and peace. Here you will come in contact with the part of yourself that is connected to the Divine.

As you learn to listen to your own internal truths, you will become less concerned with the shoulds of the world. What your neighbor thinks and the baggage you've been dragging around since childhood will take a back seat to your own internal wisdom. You will refine ways to set your attitude, consciously choose your thoughts and feelings, and stay grounded alongside other people's energies. By journey's end, you will have discovered your own true north—your life's purpose and ways to share this gift with the world.

## Tools, Meditations, and Exercises

This book is a working handbook with tools, meditations, and thought-provoking exercises intended to get your creative juices flowing. You will need a place to journal your thoughts and a quiet place to meditate. You may find that you prefer to read through a section, do the exercises, and then wait for a while before reading further. Take your time as you walk this path of discovery, and remember that the journey itself can be just as transformational as the final destination.

Some of the tools used throughout this book are part of a program of study I undertook at Boulder Psychic Institute in Boulder, Colorado. I know that for some people, the word "psychic" brings to mind wacky séances and woo-woo meditations. I had those thoughts too, yet I knew there had to be a connection between my nasty, mean inner critic voice and how I interacted with the world. I had read about the body's energy system and had a hunch that a greater understanding of auras, chakras, and the interplay between thoughts, feelings, and bodily reactions would lead to the peace and contentment I craved. So I enrolled in a beginner's program at Boulder Psychic Institute, thinking I would get out fast if it was just too silly or weird. Surprisingly, I found the program full of laughter and light, with very little psychodrama. And lo and behold, as I did the work, my inner critic stopped nagging me. Now, as a graduate student, my inner critic is almost a distant memory.

I truly believe that energy travels between people and that the thoughts and feelings of others can get stuck in our bodies, causing us to lose track of our own internal wisdom.

The first half of this book contains techniques designed to get your inner critic under control. You will learn how to clear your space of the thoughts and feelings of others, allowing more room for your own Spirit to shine through. You will craft a statement of being—a declaration of who you are, not what others think you should be. You will learn the art of saying no and how to fill your day with activities that are in alignment with your statement of being, bringing you closer to living a life full of purpose and meaning. You will come to understand how the people in your life, especially the ones who push your buttons, are here to offer clues to becoming a wiser and gentler being.

The second half of the book concentrates on how to live a life full of meaning and joy. You will discover the unique gift you are meant to share while you are on this earth and how to live your life fulfilling that purpose. You will learn how to live in a state of grace, accepting all parts of your life, even the not-so-good parts. You will set the vibration of your wants and desires by creating what I call a mock-up, then wait in certainty for your specific desire to manifest. You will also learn about the energy of money and how to use this tool (yes, money is a tool) to attract more prosperity and abundance into your life. And finally, you will put all the pieces together to discover your true life purpose and how to share that gift with the world.

At the end of every chapter, I've included energy pointers and helpful hints to enhance your learning and growth. And finally, if you find you want to delve more deeply into the topic of self-awareness, the resource section at the end of the book is full of recommendations for further study.

## Helpful Hints for Your Journey

Now that you know where we're going, let's look at how we'll get there. The following suggestions will bring in ease and grace during the process.

- Set aside a certain time and place, free from the distractions of your life, to do the daily meditation, exercises, and journaling. The more energy you devote to this process, the more you will see success reflected in your life.

- Be patient. You've had a lifetime to build up your inner critic's voice, so it might take some time to dismantle it.

- Bring an attitude of ease and play to the process. Work and effort are not prerequisites to living the life of your dreams. That's old-school thinking. The new-school way is understanding that what you think and feel you will be. You really are a magnet attracting events and circumstances into your life that are in alignment with your thoughts and feelings. So think ease, not effort. Think happy and light, not tight and tense. It's all about the be-ing, not the do-ing.

On your journey of discovery, your thoughts, feelings, beliefs, words, and actions will begin to support your life's purpose. That is the joy. That is grace. As you come to know, deep within your soul, that you are living a life full of inner purpose and meaning, you will radiate this joy out into the world, affecting everyone around you.

Let's get started.

# Part I:

# Taming Your Inner Critic

## Chapter 1

# The Energy of Should

The inner critic can be our constant companion and often our worst enemy. It can fill our world with feelings of unworthiness and self-doubt. We placate it, we cajole it, we give in to it, and we believe it!

If we stop to listen to our inner critic before we believe it, to question our internal dialogue, we might discover that some of our self-talk is not even true. The negative words coming from our inner critic could be the product of past events or could be stories people have told us about who they think we should be and what they think we should do. These shoulds may be so loud and insistent that we no longer hear the other part of our internal dialogue: our own true essence, our Spirit. This internal spirit voice, representing our Highest and Best Self, is never mean or nasty. It is our conscious connection to the Divine. It is our soul speaking directly to us.

As we learn to listen to our internal dialogue with compassion and understanding, we identify ways to differentiate our truth from the stories of others. Weeding out the critical voices, the harsh words that destroy our self-worth, allows our own internal wisdom to shine through. Through this process we come to understand our true purpose in life, discovering our life's passion and finding ways to share our unique gift with the world.

So how do the thoughts and feelings of others get buried deep within our psyche?

## Thoughts: Waves of Energy in Motion

Every thought has a specific energetic tone, a signature vibration, and the inner critic vibration is not pleasant. When our inner critic pipes up with words of criticism, our body constricts and we may feel a dramatic drop in energy. Compare this vibration to thinking of a loved one or a special time in our lives. When our body resonates with the thoughts of joy and happiness (as opposed to fear, defeat, or being overwhelmed), our body feels relaxed, spacious, and at peace.

In his book *Ageless Body, Timeless Mind,* Deepak Chopra calls a thought "an impulse of energy and information, like everything else in nature." Every person transmits energy and receives energy from others. You know this to be true because you've experienced other people's thoughts and feelings. Maybe you've walked into a room right after an argument and noticed that the energy of the room felt like you could cut it with a knife. Or maybe you've been alone in a church or a spiritual sanctuary and felt the sacredness of the space.

We've all heard stories about parents who sensed that their child, who was miles away, needed help. Or maybe you've had the experience of thinking about a person and then the phone rings. When you answer the call, your friend is on the line and says, "Hey, I just thought I'd call because I was thinking about you."

We broadcast our thoughts to our friends and neighbors and even to strangers we meet on the street. Those same people are broadcasting their thoughts on their individualized frequencies to their friends, their neighbors, and strangers they meet on the street—and to us. Thoughts are sticky. Our inner critic's voice may just be a mash-up of thoughts other people have sent our way, and unfortunately we have accepted them as truth.

So where do thoughts and feelings reside?

## Aura: The Human Energy Field

Most cultures of the world recognize that we are more than just our physical shell of skin, bones, and teeth. We are thinking, feeling, living, energetic fields of potential. We are our thoughts, feelings, emotions, brain, mind, body, and Spirit all wrapped together in a package of consciousness. All of this potential, this consciousness, doesn't just reside in the physical body. Thoughts and feelings, our own and those we've picked up from others, surround us in a personal bubble of vibrational energy called an *aura*. While this word may be new to some people, we've all experienced someone getting in our face or standing too close as we wait in line. What we are experiencing is the effect of someone invading our space, our aura.

Barbara Brennan, in her book *Hands of Light*, describes the aura as the "place where all the emotions, thoughts, memories, and behavior patterns we discuss so endlessly in therapy are located." Western scientists call this energy surrounding our bodies a *biofield*. Author and biologist Rupert Sheldrake writes about the theory of "morphic resonance," suggesting that invisible fields surround and connect all matter and allow species to communicate telepathically.

Our journey of taming the inner critic starts here, in this auric vibrational soup. Through the aura we exchange energy (thoughts, feelings, and emotions) with our fellow inhabitants of the earth. When we think of someone, we transmit some of our energy from our aura into theirs. When a parent worries about a child, they may be sending a mixture of love, concern, and judgment energy into their child's aura. A boss or co-worker may send us a little bit of criticism energy mixed in with their morning hello. These outside energies combine with our own internal truths. Soon we are unable to tell one from the other, so we accept it all, as an accurate and exact portrayal of who we truly are. This, I believe, is the genesis of the inner critic. The judgments, criticisms, and displeasure we feel about ourselves are energies we've unconsciously absorbed from people in our lives. We will work on ways to remove this unwanted energy from your aura in a moment, but the first step is always awareness.

The following exercise will help you sense this invisible space surrounding you.

---

### EXERCISE 1.1: SENSING YOUR AURA

1. Sit in a chair with your feet flat on the floor and your eyes closed.

2. Most people's auras are oval-shaped and extend about eighteen inches in all directions. Imagine this

egg-shaped space all around your body, softly pulsing with energy. You may even want to move your arms around slowly, feeling into this space around you.

3. The aura extends above your head and below your feet. Sense the space behind your knees and down to the tips of your toes. Imagine your aura extending about eighteen inches below the floor.

4. Think a peaceful thought, and imagine that peaceful energy filling your aura. Now think an angry thought and imagine your aura filled with that energy. Do you feel an energetic difference between the two?

5. Keeping your eyes closed, think a calm thought, and imagine your aura—head to toe and all around you—filled with calm, soft energy. Sit in this calm personal energy field for a moment longer. Know that as you get up and walk around, your aura moves with you.

6. When you are ready, open your eyes, get up slowly, and walk around the room.

As you begin to understand auras, you will come to the awareness that we are all connected. What affects one affects the whole. If you have ever entered a room and felt negative vibes, you have encountered some leftover energy still occupying the room. What type of energy, what thoughts and feelings, would you like to leave behind in a room? Anger and frustration, or compassion and joy? You truly are your brother's keeper, and the thoughts and feelings you transmit out into the cosmos have a lasting impact on the energy system of the entire world.

To practice seeing and feeling energies, try the following exercise the next time you are on the phone with a close friend.

---

**EXERCISE 1.2: SEEING AND FEELING ENERGIES**

1. As you speak with your friend on the phone, close your eyes and visualize your energy emanating in waves from your body. Imagine your thoughts and feelings leaving your space and traveling out, touching your friend's space.

2. Now feel your friend's thoughts coming toward you, much like a sonar wave. As your friend is talking, see if you can feel the quality of his or her vibration. Does one particular thought have a higher or lighter quality to it?

3. After you hang up the phone, close your eyes for a moment. Sit in stillness and feel the energy in the room. You may be able to sense some of your friend's energy in the space surrounding you.

## Foreign Energy: What's Yours, What's Mine?

Because we are constantly broadcasting our thoughts and feelings into the world, these thoughts travel outward and may embed in the aura of another person, affecting them in either a positive or a negative way. Likewise, the energy, thoughts, feelings, judgments, and criticisms of another person can travel and have an effect on our aura. In fact, we are bombarded daily with other people's thoughts and feelings of what they think we should do or who they think we should be. This is called *foreign energy.* Foreign energy is not bad—it is just different (foreign) from our own energy. With all these thoughts and feelings swirling around in our aura, some ours, some our neighbor's, it can become very difficult to differentiate our own hopes, wishes, and dreams from those around us. Most of our inner critic's voice is made up of this foreign energy—other people's shoulds of how they think we should behave.

The good news is that we have the ability to clean up and remove the foreign energies that have attached to our aura, thereby allowing us to hear more of our own true wisdom and internal truths. Cleaning our aura may sound a little funny, yet we brush our teeth every day, removing the foreign particles (food and bacteria) and leaving behind a fresh, clean mouth. The same is true of our aura. Cleaning the aura will remove foreign energy, allowing our unique thoughts and feelings to shine.

We often clean our aura without even realizing it. Maybe you've walked away from a particularly offensive conversation by literally shaking out both hands or shrugging your shoulders to remove the icky after-effects of your conversation. On the other hand, you might have felt like rinsing off in the shower or shaking your body, much like a wet dog coming out of the river. Either way, you were unconsciously removing foreign energy from your aura.

Of course, not all encounters with foreign energy are as dramatic. Simply brushing the energy off your arms, legs, head, and back as if you were removing a layer of dust from your skin might be sufficient. Or you might literally expel foreign energy from your body by inhaling deeply and then exhaling through your mouth with force. These methods work well if you are consciously aware of picking up energies from others and wish to expel the energy right away.

However, we're not always consciously aware of exchanging energies with people in our environment. In this case, it might be helpful to use a tool that, once activated, will continue to work the entire day, keeping your energy system free of other people's thoughts and feelings. This tool, called a *grounding cord*, is an energy cable that connects you securely to the center of the earth. Through the force of gravity, it efficiently drains any energy from your body and your aura that is not your own.

A grounding cord can be visualized as any object. A strong rope with an anchor on the end, a hollow beam of light, or a stretch of silk are all visuals that I use at varying times, depending on my mood. The most important thing to remember is that this tube of energy will automatically carry foreign energy out of your body, depositing it deep within the earth's core.

Attaching your aura, as well as your body, to this grounding cord allows your full energetic system to be connected to the earth. Your aura surrounds your body and extends out about eighteen inches in all directions, including below your feet. When I first started grounding, I found it a little odd to think about my aura extending below the floor. I had to step out of my three-dimensional view of things and remember that energy is like air: it exists whether I can see it or not. As I let my mind accept this idea, without trying to analyze it, I could then picture this area below my feet where my grounding cord and aura meet. In fact, as I set the intent for the two to merge together, I could actually feel them fusing together, forming an airtight seal.

The following exercise may help to cement this visual in place.

---

### EXERCISE 1.3: RELEASING FOREIGN ENERGY
### THROUGH YOUR GROUNDING CORD

1. Sit in a chair with your feet flat on the floor and your eyes closed. Take a couple of deep breaths and imagine a wide, hollow tube of energy—a grounding cord—out in front of your closed eyes. Now imagine attaching the grounding cord to your body, where your hips and thighs meet (figure 1). Feel the weight of the cord around your body as it draws you deeper into your chair.

2. Imagine this field of energy falling from your hips, below your feet, and through the floor, and continuing down to the center of the planet. Visualize it falling below the earth's crust, below the rocks, the minerals, into the core of the earth. Imagine hearing the thud as the grounding cord hits the earth's center, anchoring in place. Feel a slight upward tug as it lets you know that it is completely anchored and secure.

3. Picture your aura around your body. See it enveloping your physical body in a cocoon of pulsing, vibrating energy. Imagine this bubble of energy extending above your head and below your feet. Bring your awareness to the area below your feet, where your aura meets your grounding cord. Imagine fusing your aura to your grounding cord, making an airtight seal.

Know that any foreign energy in your aura will now be able to drain down your grounding cord.

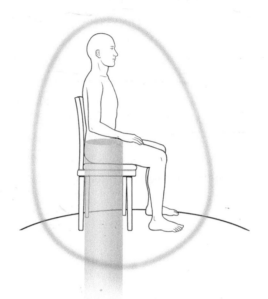

*Figure 1: Grounding to the Earth*

4. Bring your awareness to a place in your body where you feel some tension, perhaps your shoulders or your feet. Now intend for the tension to release. As it does so, imagine the energetic tension dropping out of your body and aura and falling down the grounding cord. Give your body permission to release all that stress, all that foreign energy. You don't need to store it in your system. Release it all. Imagine all that energy returning to the earth. Watch it dissipate.

5. Take a couple of deep breaths. Slowly open your eyes, get up, and walk around. Notice that your grounding cord is still in place, anchoring you to the planet. Some people immediately feel a little bit more focused and centered when they stand. Others notice a more pronounced feeling when seated. Know that your grounding cord is attached whether you feel it or not.

This grounding cord stays in place the entire day, continually draining out all the gunk in your aura and returning it to the earth. Anytime you begin to feel tired, scattered, anxious, or annoyed, imagine this grounding cord removing those toxic thoughts and feelings from your body and your aura.

## Calling Back Your Life Force

Energy, in the form of thoughts and feelings, has the ability to travel. When we find ourselves thinking of a work project late into the evening hours, our body may be at home, but some part of us is still hanging around our office, desk, or computer. Most people have an inordinate amount of their life force scattered about in the past, in the future, with their sick friend, or anywhere but in the present moment. If we are constantly planning our future life, we've sent some of our life force off into the future. When our head is full of the argument we just had with a neighbor, we may be hanging out in their aura as foreign energy. By calling our own energies back to us, we remove the energy we've inadvertently left in our friend's space, allowing them to become more of who they are—and we do the same for

become more potent beings. We do this by
...alled the *golden sun*.

...n sun has two functions. One is to call back
...force so we can function at our full potential.
...to offer us a way to replace the foreign energies
leaving our body via the grounding cord with energies that
are more in alignment with who we truly are. When we *fill
in* our aura with energies such as peace, love, and self-acceptance, we dilute the power of the lower-vibrational energies (fear, anger, resentment), offering us one more way
to tame our inner critic.

The grounding cord and the golden sun are what I call
foundational tools. We will use them throughout the rest of
the book, so you might want to bookmark these pages for
easy reference.

---

### EXERCISE 1.4:

#### FILLING IN YOUR AURA WITH A GOLDEN SUN

1. Sit quietly with your feet on the floor and your eyes
   closed. Take a couple of deep breaths. Imagine a
   gigantic golden sun, about three times the size of
   your body, above your head. See the sun filled with
   golden light. Now place a giant magnet in this sun,
   and ask the magnet to call back your scattered energy
   from past events and from time spent at your job or
   with family and friends. Feel all that energy zoom
   back into the golden sun.

2. Imagine that energy being cleansed and restored to
   the frequency that's just right for your body. This is
   your life force energy.

3. Next, fill this golden sun with relaxation, peace, abundance, self-validation, or whatever qualities would most benefit you in this moment. See those qualities permeate the sun, vibrating at a frequency that's just right for your body.

4. Now imagine reaching up and popping the golden sun. Let the deflated sun's beneficial qualities flow into your aura and fill in every cell and membrane of your body.

5. Feel yourself refreshed and enveloped in a cocoon of energies that are just right for you today. The world around you can be full of chaos and turmoil, but when you're filled with your own energy, you can be relaxed and free from stress and turmoil.

6. Sit in this wonderfully peaceful space of relaxation and fullness for a moment or two. When you are ready, open your eyes and notice how you feel. Your body may be vibrating a little bit faster, or you may feel a bit more focused or all here.

When you are full of yourself, filled to the brim with your own unique life force energy, there's less room in your aura for foreign energy. Isn't that cool?

## Meditation: Listening to Your Spirit

A daily practice of grounding to the earth and visualizing your aura full of your own unique energies will help you differentiate the thoughts and feelings of others from your own true wisdom. As foreign energy leaves your aura and body and is replaced by missing parts of yourself that you left sprinkled around in past conversations and future planning, you become more of who you truly are. As you do this, the voice of your inner critic subsides, allowing the voice of your inner guidance system, your Spirit, to come forth.

This process of change does not occur on a superficial level of wishing it into being, nor does is happen by waving a magic wand and having our inner critic disappear in a cloud of smoke. It involves exploring, discovering, and bringing awareness to our deepest, most profound beliefs about life. Then, and only then, can we shift the energy patterning, aligning ourselves with our own true wisdom and revealing the answers to living a life of purpose. Meditation offers us this opportunity to explore the inner world of our knowingness.

If you tried meditation in the past but found that your inner dialogue was a distraction, a form of creative visualization may be a good beginning point. Instead of waiting for your inner voice to be silent, you actively engage your mind in picturing what you want. Sometimes your intuition will show you a picture in your mind's eye. Other times you may hear, or just know, certain words or phrases.

The words *visualize* and *imagine* mean different things to different people. If I ask you to close your eyes and imagine yourself on a hot summer day sipping lemonade as you lie in the backyard hammock, the first step is to picture this in your mind. As you do that, your body might feel relaxed and you might sense the peace and tranquility of summer afternoons. You might even imagine the sensation of the tart yet sweet lemonade hitting the back of your throat. You know that you are not really experiencing this imagined scene, yet on an emotional level you are creating the experience of relaxation and peace. By consciously picturing a relaxing scene in your mind, you are aligning yourself with the energetic vibration of relaxation and peace, thereby consciously experiencing the feelings and emotions as if you were physically swaying in your backyard hammock.

I believe that when we close our eyes and imagine or visualize something, we're actually using our inner sight, our clairvoyance. When you utilize your imagination in the following exercise—and in the other exercises throughout this book—you're not creating a fairy-tale, made-up experience. As you picture your grounding cord or imagine all your own energies zooming back into a golden sun, you are creating the experience of being grounded to the earth, with your scattered energies flowing into your body on an energetic level. This is actually happening; you just can't see it with your physical eyes. As we sit in meditation and let go of the need to see with our physical eyes, we tune in to our inner world of knowingness, our Spirit, our connection to the Divine.

One of the first steps in any meditation is getting yourself centered and present. Being centered means to be in present time, right here, right now; you're not thinking of what happened in the past or about tomorrow's to-do list. When you're scattered, you're less potent and unable to bring your full potential to the task at hand. So centering becomes a practice of mindfulness, being fully present, with all your thoughts and feelings in one place.

This place of stillness is the home of our Spirit. It is located between our ears, behind our eyes, in the center of our head. (It is the middle of our sixth chakra, our seat of intuition; see chapter 5 for a discussion of the chakras.) We will practice being in the center of our head and connected to the earth in the following meditation.

---

### EXERCISE 1.5: GROUNDING MEDITATION

1. Sit with your eyes closed, feet flat on the floor.

2. Take a couple of deep breaths and become aware of your breath flowing in and out, in and out. With your eyes closed, feel your body come to stillness as you sink a little bit deeper into your chair.

3. Bring all of your awareness to the center of your head. Between your ears, behind your eyes, and in the center of your head is your personal space, your sanctuary. Be there now. If you feel that the thoughts of the day or the energies of past events are still with you, just become aware of those thoughts and then ask them to leave. It's that simple. Ask the thoughts of the day to step out of your private space. Feel them leave. Watch as wisps of energy move out of the way. Close the door to this space and be alone.

4. Relax and just be.

5. Now imagine a wide tube of energy connected to the base of your spine. This is your grounding cord. Feel the weight of it around your body as you cinch it in place.

6. Imagine this tube falling below your feet, through the floor, and continuing down to the center of the planet. Feel this tube of energy anchoring into the core of the earth. Feel a slight upward tug as it lets you know it is completely anchored and secure. You might feel yourself sink a little bit deeper into your chair as your grounding cord begins to drain out the foreign energy in your body.

7. Next, imagine your aura enveloping your physical body in a cocoon of pulsing, vibrating energy. Picture the area below your feet, where your grounding cord and aura meet. Imagine your aura fusing to your grounding cord, making an airtight seal.

8. Inhale and exhale. Feel safe, secure, and at peace. On the exhale, feel yourself sink deeper into your chair as you release any excess baggage: the thoughts and shoulds of others. Let all that baggage flow down through the grounding cord to the center of the earth.

9. Next, imagine a large golden sun above your head. Place a huge magnet in that sun. Ask the magnet to call all of your own energy back from wherever you might have left it. You might have left some of your energy in a conversation from last night or in a thought about a future event. Feel your energies zoom back into this golden sun.

10. Imagine all that energy being cleansed and restored to the frequency that is just right for your body.

11. Next, fill the golden sun with relaxation, peace, abundance, self-validation, or whatever qualities would benefit you most in this moment. See those qualities permeate the sun, vibrating at a frequency that is in perfect alignment with your system.

12. Imagine reaching up and popping the golden sun. Feel all that clean, fresh energy enter the top of your head and travel throughout your body. Feel the golden sun energy reach the tips of your fingers and toes. Feel your body tingle with the infusion of this refreshing energy. Feel the energy surge out into your aura, filling you up completely with energies of your choosing.

13. Be refreshed and enveloped in a cocoon of vibrations that are just right for you today. The world around you can be full of chaos and turmoil, but you, filled up with your own energy, can be relaxed and free from stress.

14. Sit in this wonderfully peaceful space of relaxation and fullness for a moment or two.

15. Before you leave this meditative space, ask your grounding cord to stay attached for the rest of the day, continually releasing foreign energy from your body and aura and keeping you connected to the earth. When you are ready, open your eyes and come out of meditation.

You can return to the meditation many times during the day to check in with your grounding cord and aura, knowing they will be working to keep your system clean and clear, whether you are consciously aware of them or not.

By spending time like this each day, we are laying the foundation for taming our inner critic and living a life full of purpose and meaning. So far on our journey of discovery, we've established that the thoughts, feelings, judgments, criticisms, and shoulds of the world (foreign energies) form the basis of our internally destructive mind chatter. We've become conscious of our aura and discovered ways to remove foreign energy from our space. We also understand that by calling back our own energies through the use of the golden sun, we allow ourselves to be more fully present in our lives. Removing foreign energy and filling in our aura with our own life force are both prerequisites to soothing the internal voice of unreason. In the next chapter, we will discuss specific techniques to permanently remove some of this negative self-talk.

## Energy Pointers

- Think of your daily meditation time as your special treat to yourself—it offers you loads of renewed vitality and energy, without artificial stimulants such as caffeine or sugar.

- Play a game with yourself the next time you are seated next to someone. See if you can sense where that person's aura ends.

- Energy can be light and playful or heavy and draggy. See if you can sense those energies attached to some of the words you speak.

## Helpful Hints

- Add some extra zing to your next workout session by filling in with golden suns during class. Your instructor may wonder where all your extra energy came from.

- Play a game of telepathy with a friend. See if you can sense each other's thoughts. You'll be surprised at what you intuit.

- One day imagine your grounding cord as a hollow tree trunk. Another day imagine it as a tube of golden light. Have fun playing with different images. There is no right or wrong way, just your way.

## Chapter 2

# Releasing Negative Self-Talk

As we tune in to our inner world through daily meditation, and as we replace the thoughts and feelings of others with our own truth, we may discover that the story of who we think we are is just that—a story. Our internalized picture of ourselves may have evolved from some very early childhood experiences. This core life story may be filled with our parents' hopes and dreams for us, our neighbors' judgments about what children should do and be, and society's rules of how people should behave. All of these outside influences color how we see the world and our place in it, and subsequently how we live. This story forms the basis of our internal dialogue. In order to tame our inner critic, it's important to understand the root cause of these thoughts and feelings.

The following exercise will help to bring your core life story to the surface of your awareness so you can examine it, keep the powerful statements that work for you, and let go of those parts that no longer serve you. In this exercise, we use a technique often called *mind mapping*—a way of jotting down free associations. You'll refer to this exercise over and over again, so you might want to highlight these instructions and record your initial work in your journal or on a piece of paper so you'll be able to easily retrieve your work for future reference.

---

### EXERCISE 2.1: THE NAME WEB: WHO DO YOU THINK YOU ARE?

1. Draw a circle in the middle of the page and write your name in that circle. Now start writing down your associations with this word. Do this by drawing lines moving outward from your name. An association is any word or phrase that pops into your mind when you think about yourself.

2. Record both the positive and negative associations. You may find that a word triggers connections to other words or ideas. Write these down too, allowing one idea to flow freely into the next.

3. When you run out of associations, return to the center circle with your name in it and see if more associations come to mind. Do this exercise quickly; don't edit your thoughts.

4. You might reflect upon:

    - what you like most about being you.

    - some of your mother's favorite phrases she used in describing you while you were growing up.

- some of the descriptive words you use to describe yourself, such as being too shy, too short, or having a beautiful smile.

- phrases that your inner critic uses to describe you, such as "I'm so dumb," "I'm not good enough," or "I'm afraid they'll find out my secret."

- phrases your best friend might use to describe you, such as "You're so compassionate," "You listen well," or "You always say exactly what you mean."

5. After you've finished, you'll have something that looks like a big web or net. Some associations will form clusters full of descriptive words, while others will stand alone.

6. Draw circles around the words with a repetitive tone or mood. You might find themes of unworthiness, resentment, or confusion. On the positive side, you might find themes of spontaneity or empathy. Other energies, such as love, health, or creativity, may be mentioned. Write those repeating themes off to the side of your web.

This picture, or name web, with all of its associations and intricacies, is your personal model of how you see yourself operating in the world. This structure of knowing serves as a filter in every conversation or thought you have.

## Tools to Remove Negative Self-Talk

As you review your name web, reflect upon whether there were phrases on your web that surprised you. Often, our parents and friends unknowingly send a thought or opinion our way, and we accept it into our space. This thought sticks in our aura, becoming part of the story of how we see ourselves. This is foreign energy. It's a thought or feeling of what someone else wants us to be.

Foreign energy does not always appear as negative. If your mother told you that you were a beautiful baby, then that thought may have imbedded in your aura. It may even have found its way onto your name web and had a major impact on the way you see yourself. While we might label this as good foreign energy, it is still someone else's opinion. It could be that your mother, while telling you that you were a beautiful baby, thought to herself, "I want her to be perfect." Both intertwined energies came into your space, possibly affecting your internal dialogue. As a result, your inner critic may become loud and insistent when you are not perfect. Removing all foreign energies from your system, even the seemingly good vibes, allows room for your own Spirit to shine through. In our work together, we will concentrate first on the phrases that are obviously negative.

To start, let's work a fairly tame phrase, one that doesn't trigger much emotion in your body but still has a negative connotation. Look back over your name web and find such a phrase. Then do the following exercise.

## EXERCISE 2.2: WHOSE VOICE IS THAT?

1. Pick a phrase to work on from your name web. Say the phrase aloud. As you speak that phrase, close your eyes and visualize the experience. Remember who was there and what they said to you.

2. You may find that this is the voice of your mother, a teacher, or the bully on the elementary school playground. Just understanding and acknowledging whom that voice belongs to can dilute its power. Remember that this is foreign energy; someone gave you that tag, said that word to you, put that picture in your aura. It is not actually your thought. This is not how you honestly feel about *you*; this is what someone else said, perhaps long ago.

3. Release that thought and let it flow out of your body, never to return to your space. Let go of that energy. Shake it off, brush it off, or expel it with a swoosh of your breath. Watch it drain down your grounding cord, never to return. It is someone else's thought about who you should be or what you should do.

4. Try this exercise on a couple more of your name-web associations.

5. Become aware of all the energy, both positive and negative, that we exchange with the people in our lives.

6. Fill in your aura with words of self-love and self-acceptance.

Once you have figured out whose voice is in your head, some of those negative comments will lose their power and melt away into the ether, never to be heard again.

Pick another phrase from your name web that you are ready to explore. Close your eyes and say the phrase out loud. Imagine a ball of energy representing this phrase forming in front of your closed eyes. Spend a moment just looking at that ball of energy. Don't discount what you see. Remember that this form of creative visualization involves using your intuition in new ways.

As you visualize the words of your phrase, see them forming a colorful mass of waves of oscillating energy. Next, imagine moving that ball of energy down to the floor by your right foot. Watch it move to the floor. With your eyes still closed, imagine looking down at your right foot and seeing this big ball of energy representing the phrase from your name web. Check out the colors of the energy. See it as a big glob of goo on the floor. Acknowledge that this phrase is no longer true for you. It is a story of what someone else thought you should do or be. It is another person's judgment: a criticism of you. It is not your own truth. You don't need to hold this foreign energy in your body any longer. When you decide that you're ready to let this energy go, *step on it.* Stomp on it. Smash it to smithereens! Or, if that is a little too violent for you, just tell it to go away. Watch as that big ball of someone else's energy disappears. Have fun with this. Make it a game. Release those negative thoughts from your internal dialogue.

One of my clients, Donna, had an interesting experience as she worked on her name web. One of the phrases on Donna's name web was "Don't rock the boat." She remembered being reprimanded many times by her mother for voicing a contrary opinion. She puzzled over why her mother would have felt that way, and then it came to her. She remembered her mother's stories of growing up in a household with an alcoholic father whose moods were to be feared. Donna's mother learned not to rock the boat as a child, choosing instead to become passive and adopt a get-along-at-all-costs attitude.

Recalling these stories, Donna realized that her mother's words were leftover memories from a childhood in which rocking the boat had dire consequences. Once the story became clear, it was easy for Donna to release this energy from her space. She chose to allow the voice of her mother saying "don't rock the boat" to slide out of her body and to place this energy down on the floor. As she looked at the colors of this energy, she noticed some sickly green and yellow colors that reminded her of a slowly healing bruise. Because she felt some compassion for her mother, Donna chose to have the blob of gooey energy melt away instead of stomping it out. As she did this, she felt a part of her heart open up. She also felt a distinct shift, a letting-go sensation, occur in her abdomen. She knew that a part of her inner critic had just been tamed.

Quieting your inner critic is a process. Remember that this inner voice of unreason has been around for a long time and is not going to be calmed in one day. With that said, remember to bring some lightness and ease to the exercises. Energy moves out of the way once we become conscious of it. Awareness and intent are the keys—not effort or drama. Be in ease and lightness as you move out the old energies.

As you begin to move deeper into some of the stickier phrases on your name web, the work will become a little more intense. You might want to return to this exercise over and over as we continue to do our work together.

Some of the most cruel and destructive energies are jealousy, shame, and invalidation. They hide behind the judgment and value statements that others, either consciously or unconsciously, throw at us. These are the shoulds of life: "I think you should be this" or "Why aren't you more like so and so?" When parents are teaching a child to be safe in the world, they often inadvertently send this energy toward the one they love most. Parents may say, "We want more for you. We want you to be better than we are, smarter than we are, or richer than we are. We love you and want more for you."

While our parents' intention is one thing, their message may be another. The energy being transmitted to the child is: "You are not enough," "You need to change," "My love is conditional love," "If you were different, I would love you more," or "You are damaged and we need to fix you." Shame is a result of not living up to these sorts of expectations. You feel small, less than, unworthy, like you don't belong to the group.

Soon we'll do an exercise to work on the energy of comparison or invalidation, but first I want to share one of my own childhood stories. I grew up in a splintered family. My grandmother and great-aunt did not communicate with each other, although they lived on the same block in a very small town. My father and mother tried to stay out of the drama, but the family stories of dislike filtered down to my sisters and me. I heard how my great-aunt often used her gregarious, charming personality as a weapon against my grandmother. So when my father turned to me one night and said, "You are too much like your Great-Aunt A," I was devastated. That comparison energy hit me in the gut and sent me into an emotional spiral. I was maybe ten—and all I knew was that I was damaged. Somehow I had an unacceptable personality trait. I didn't know what that trait was (is charming bad?), but I knew I was being labeled as unacceptable. I wasn't loved for myself; I was too much like my great-aunt. I was being told to change.

Maybe you've had a similar experience. Perhaps there's a circle, or several circles, on your name web with a statement that's your version of "You are too much like your great-aunt." Statements like these are the big, ugly, nasty voices, full of unworthiness and not-belonging energy. This type of inner criticism will not go away on its own. It's sticky and stubborn and forms the centerpiece of the most vicious parts of our internal dialogue.

## The Tapping Technique

Let's tackle one of those insistent tapes playing in your head by using a technique called *tapping*. Tapping is a simple, effective tool somewhere between hypnosis, meditation, and acupressure that was first used by Roger Callahan, PhD, in the early 1980s. Callahan called it Thought Field Therapy (TFT). One of Callahan's students, Gary Craig, developed a similar system of tapping that he called Emotional Freedom Technique (EFT). Since then, tapping has been widely recommended as an effective technique to remove energy blocks. Recently the American Psychological Association (APA) granted continuing education credits for psychologists to study tapping, also known as energy psychology. Tapping is widely used by energy medicine practitioners, such as Donna Eden, and other professionals, including Joseph Mercola, an osteopathic physician (DO) and natural health practitioner.

Tapping moves the energy associated with a belief, releasing it from the body. When you tap, you say the belief aloud to bring up the corresponding emotion in the nervous system. Then you tap what we call *meridian points* to reset the system (see figure 2). Each meridian point is at the end of a nerve channel in the body. Tapping sends a shockwave down that channel that clears out the emotion residing there. When the emotion is gone, your mind no longer attaches to the belief. Suddenly your mind is free to reprocess your emotional response, turning a negative into a positive. I know it might be hard to believe, so hang with me for a moment and try this for yourself in the next exercise. Seeing—or in this case, feeling—is believing.

Before you begin tapping, you will rate the strength of a belief. After a round of tapping, you will rate it again. Zero on the scale corresponds to zero emotional responses in your body when you say your belief or tell your story. Ten signals a strong emotional reaction. You'll continue tapping until you're down to one or zero on the scale.

After tapping out the negative, you'll tap in a positive replacement feeling. Once your system is at a neutral point (one or zero on the rating scale), you can charge it up with some empowering, joyful energy and beliefs, which will allow you to attract the positive life experiences you desire.

Before you start the tapping exercise, let's go over a few details. First, you will choose a particularly painful theme or phrase from your name web—one that's not serving you well. Then you will recall some of your childhood or young-adult experiences associated with this belief. You will use this negative theme and all the emotion attached to it as your base tapping experience. You will be bringing up not-so-good feelings, but this is actually how you will clear them from your system. During the exercise, you will also speak these memories out loud. This will enable you to relive the experience with all the rich, though painful, emotions you felt at the time. And while you're focusing on these negative thoughts, you will be tapping gently and rhythmically on specific parts of your body.

Let's say that on your name web you have written the statement "I'm too fat." While reflecting on this statement, you recall an incident in seventh-grade gym class when some of the other girls were giggling and smirking in your direction. You overhead one of them say, "She's as fat as a pig." You were devastated. Although you may not have been fat at all, the words stuck, and they implanted so deeply in your psyche that you began a diet immediately. To this day, you have never liked your body and have always felt fat. Use this or another phrase from your own name web in the following exercise.

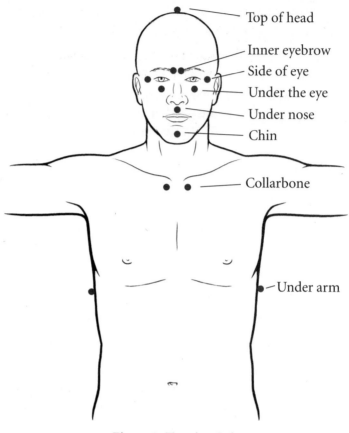

*Figure 2: Tapping Points*

**EXERCISE 2.3: TAPPING TO RELEASE EMOTIONAL PAIN**
For this exercise, you'll need a quiet space where you can be alone for a while. Have your name web and your notebook with you.

1. Look at your name web and pick a really painful phrase. On a scale of zero to ten, with ten being the

strongest, rate the strength of the emotion attached to that belief. Write that number down.

2. Now recall an incident or situation associated with this belief. Evaluate what happened, who was there, how you felt, and the emotions you experienced that day. State the negative belief aloud, bringing up all the associated emotions.

3. Now start tapping the meridian points as you tell the story (see figure 2). Tap five to seven times on each of the points in the following order:

   a. Eyebrow at the inside corner of your eye

   b. The outside corner of your eye

   c. Under the eye

   d. Under the nose

   e. Center of the chin

   f. Inside the collarbone, close to the larynx

   g. Under the arm

   h. The top of your head

   i. Go back to the eyebrow point and start the sequence again

4. It doesn't matter whether you tap fast or slow, hard or soft. Just find your own rhythm and let the story flow.

5. As you tap, talk about whatever comes to mind about the belief you're focusing on. Remember how you felt, the thoughts that ran through your head, and the decisions you made. Speak the story as if

you were telling your best friend what happened that day.

6. Take a moment to rate your belief again. Give it a rating between one and ten. If your belief registers higher than a one, do another round of tapping. Your story may shift as you continue tapping. The "I'm way too fat" story might morph into statements such as "I'm not good enough" or "No one likes me." That's fine; just let it out. Getting to your core issues is like peeling the layers of an onion. Rate your feeling again after this second round of tapping.

7. Keep tapping the meridian points until the story feels complete. It could take five or six rounds of tapping—perhaps more. Continue with as many rounds as you need, until the negative belief—in this case, "I'm too fat"—releases. You might feel an actual shift in your body as your negative belief releases.

8. After you feel you have tapped out the negative, it is time to tap in the positive. Review your name web for some positive phrases. Bring to mind the feelings associated with the positive phrases. Some examples might be "I love my body just the way it is right now," "I am perfect just the way I am," "I accept this new, positive belief with joy and appreciation," or "I love the calm and peace that I feel now."

9. Do a couple more rounds of tapping with the positive affirmations using the same sequence of meridian points. This will fill your system with

affirming energy and solidify the positive energy in your system.

It might take several subsequent tapping sessions to shift a negative belief, because there are many layers to the beliefs we hold. Even if you tap it down to a zero one day, you may wake up the next day and experience a higher rating. That doesn't mean the previous tapping didn't work. What's happening is that the next layer of negativity, fear, or lack is surfacing. To have life-transforming results from tapping, it's important to be diligent and patient. You truly can tap out the negative and tap in the positive.

## Destroying Foreign Energy

By now you know that most of the negative voices of your inner critic belong to someone else; they're not truly yours. The messages from those voices are foreign energies residing in your system, in your aura. Remember that what you think and feel emanates from you out into the cosmos. One of the universal laws is this: like attracts like. You really are a giant magnet attracting to you events and circumstances that are in alignment with your current set of thoughts and feelings. This is why it's so critical to remove the negative self-talk and replace it with positive statements about what makes you special.

Tapping is a great way to release some of the deep emotional pain we all experience, but you probably don't want to sit in public tapping on meridian points and speaking your story out loud! This next tool, blowing up a rose, is taught at Boulder Psychic Institute's Enlightenment Program, and it's a method I've incorporated into my daily routine to help remove foreign energies from my space. I especially enjoy using this tool because it's so visceral. I can actually feel energy leaving my body and aura and see it being blown to pieces in my imagination.

---

### EXERCISE 2.4: BLOWING UP A ROSE

Our inner critic's voice is a mixture of all the foreign energies (the shoulds, expectations, judgments, and criticisms) we've accepted as our own truth. By cleaning these energies out of our space, we make room for our own Spirit's voice to be heard. Some of this foreign energy leaves via our grounding cord, some of it is removed by tapping on our meridian points, and some of it we can call out of our body and explode into tiny bits of energetic dust. Follow along as I explain how to blow up a rose.

1. Close your eyes and take a couple of deep breaths. Imagine a rose floating in front of your closed eyes. The rose can be any color, shape, and size. In fact, if you don't like roses, then pick another flower or any symbol that feels comfortable to you.

2. Next, visualize a giant magnet in the middle of this rose.

3. Recall one of the phrases on your name web that is no longer true for you. Perhaps it was something like "I am so stupid," and you remember a certain subject in school that never made sense to you.

4. Acknowledge that the story ("I am so stupid") is false. You may not have understood the subject matter of a certain class, but that doesn't make you stupid.

5. Ask the magnet in your rose to pull your story toward it. Watch as each piece of your story leaves your body and moves away from you and into the rose. Watch the streams of color as they leave your heart, throat, and mind. Watch as the colors move into the rose. See how the rose grows bigger and bigger as the pieces of the story stick to the magnet. Feel yourself growing lighter and lighter as all this excess baggage leaves your energy field.

6. When the magnet has removed as much of your negative story or self-talk as possible, blow up the rose. Watch it disintegrate, and feel the story disintegrate too.

7. Now that you've removed some foreign energy from yourself, you'll want to fill in the gaps with energies that are in alignment with who you are right now. To do this, visualize a golden sun above your head. Ask for this golden sun to fill in with all of your own life force energy that you've left scattered in past or future events. Visualize bits of energy filling up this golden sun. Next, add some self-validation, worthiness, peace, or whatever energy feels good to you in this moment. Let those energies infuse the golden sun, and watch it grow in size. When you're ready, pop the golden sun and feel all those warm, validating energies flood into the crown of your head and cascade throughout your body.

8. Sit with all this wonderful energy for a moment, then come out of meditation.

You may have noticed that the energy moving into the rose was full of color. All energy (including thoughts and feelings) is continually vibrating and assumes the color belonging to that specific rate of vibration. Different energies vibrate at different rates. Anger, frustration, and resistance vibrate at a lower rate than joy, peace, and love. You might be "feeling blue" or "seeing red," which are on the lower end of the vibration spectrum. On the other hand, you might see joy as a sunny yellow or love as a soft pink, and you might feel those energies vibrating at a higher rate.

Part of the work we will do in healing your inner critic is ferreting out some of the lower-vibrational energies and replacing them with higher vibrations more in alignment with your Spirit. Begin to notice what the energy of peace looks like to you. Maybe it's soft pink or pale sea-foam green. Check out the color of worthiness. Maybe you see a pale yellow or a soft, gentle green. Each person interprets this marriage of color to emotion differently, so begin to understand your color palette of emotions and their corresponding energies.

As you move out the lower-vibrational energies by blowing up a rose, tapping, or sending the energy down your grounding cord, you defuse the power of a story you've been telling yourself. You replace the negative internal dialogue with energies that are more current, more authentic. So blow up some roses. Stomp on some negative self-talk. Tap on a story that no longer holds your truth.

Spend some time clearing out the negatives that no longer work for you. Nurture yourself.

The next step, which we'll cover in the following chapter, will be to bring in positive energy to replace all the negative thoughts and feelings that you have removed.

## Energy Pointers

- What color is the energy of joy to you? What is the color of the energy of anger? Begin to build your own library of associations.

- In your daily meditation, visualize what the center of the earth looks like. Is it full of light, or is it full of scary monsters? Do you see other grounding cords down there?

## Helpful Hints

- Giving your inner critic a name, such as Annoying Alan or Angry Alice, brings an added lightness to this very heavy energy.

- Share with your best friend how to smash an energy to smithereens. Laugh, have fun, and be in joy and playfulness as you smash and tap and explode those energies that are not working for you.

## Chapter 3

# Bringing in the Positive

Thoughts and feelings are extremely powerful. One of the universal truths is that like attracts like. What we think and feel we will be. If our inner critic is running on an automatic loop of negativity, then we can't help but draw to us events and circumstances that are a vibrational match. That's not what we want! As we work to tame the inner critic, let's also decide to replace the internal fault-finding with words, thoughts, and feelings that are more reflective of our true nature. The following exercise is a great way to tap into your Spirit and bring forth what I call *heart traits*, or qualities that reflect the true nature of your essence. You will then craft those traits into a statement of being, a declaration of who you truly are.

Heart traits are mirrors into your soul. They are reflections of your Highest and Best Self. It is Spirit speaking directly to you and reminding you that you are a spark of that Divine Light, so uniquely special that no one else in the entire galaxy can shine as brilliantly as you can. As you become aware of these traits, know that they are a true reflection of the best of you. They help to capture and harness energy of that same vibration, allowing you to fulfill your life purpose. The following exercises, which were adapted from Dr. Maria Nemeth's book *The Energy of Money*, will help you tap into these traits, acknowledge them as yours, and begin the process of living a fuller, richer life.

---

### EXERCISE 3.1: FINDING TRAITS
### THAT WARM YOUR HEART

1. In your journal, list your best qualities. List the attributes as they pop into your mind. You might be good at being a friend or being considerate. You might be good at figuring out puzzles or maintaining calm during an emergency. You might be able to see humor in the direst of circumstances. You might be good at telling the truth, even when it's uncomfortable, or you might have a talent for caring for friends or neighbors when they are sick. You might be a patient, attentive listener. The key is that the feeling resonates deeply within you.

2. Let's take the example of "I am kind." As you wrote the words "I am kind," you may have recalled instances in which you were *not* particularly kind. In that case, the feelings associated with "kind" might include some lack or doubt. Notice whose voice you hear speaking those words of lack or doubt. It's probably not your own voice. Feel beneath the first response as you say the word "kind" aloud. If you smile and feel a warm, soft excitement in your heart as you say

the word, then the answer is *yes*. Circle that word. If, on the other hand, you get a lukewarm response to the question, don't despair. The lukewarm response just means that this is not one of your top traits. After all, we are all different, and there is no judgment involved in this exercise. It is not about a right or wrong answer, it just is. Accept it, then go forth and find those traits that truly do warm your heart right to the core.

3. Next, bring to mind a person you admire (a friend, family member, former teacher, coach, etc.), along with the qualities the individual possesses that bring a smile to your face. Traits such as loyalty, honesty, intelligence, courage, creativeness, adventurousness, kindness, or gentleness might come to mind. Write those traits in your journal and again, do the same test. If this trait warms your heart center and makes you smile, then circle it. Like attracts like. Know that you are attracted to those who are most like you. Yes, it's okay to say this: *I am great and I attract people with qualities that match my own.* If you admire your friend because she is so caring toward her mother, remember that like attracts like and that you possess that same quality of caring for others.

4. Look back over your name web. Add any positive traits that resonate with you to your growing list of heart traits. Look at each personal quality and circle it if it truly resonates with you.

5. Don't worry about whether you have a few good traits or many. The point is to find those that are

most true for you. Look at the circled words again. This is your Spirit talking directly to you, telling you how special and unique you are. Make a new list of your circled words, and at the top write:

## Heart Traits: Messages from Spirit reminding me of WHO I REALLY AM

This is the core of your personal power. The traits you listed are part of your nature. Accept them, love them, and honor them. Become familiar with the words. Memorize them. Validate them.

Our primary purpose in life is to remember who we really are and to live our life on purpose. Accept that your heart traits are qualities you possess. Be comfortable with the thought that you are a terrific person on the inside with fantastic qualities waiting to shine through. Own these qualities. Make them a part of your inner core. They represent the true you.

If you are having difficulties accepting these qualities as your own, spend some time considering what might be blocking your way. You might be having issues with feeling worthy of these qualities. Most of us have quite a difficult time loving ourselves and accepting our Highest and Best Self for what it is: a true reflection of our connection to the Divine. Remember that your thoughts emanate out into the world. Reflect upon the quality of the energy you are currently sending into space. Your vibrational frequency is in tune with your thoughts and feelings. Let your frequency be the best and highest it can be. Pull out your list of heart traits. Read the list of qualities you possess and validate them. Honor them and accept them. Live them.

You may find there's a nagging voice in the back of your head saying, "You don't really believe you're *that* special, do you?" Sit in silence with that thought and name that voice. Remember who said that to you and under what circumstances. Use the tapping method for that negative experience. Release it. Then, after you have tapped out the negative, tap in the positive. Read your heart trait list to yourself as you tap, tap, tap in the positive, wonderful, love-filled, heartwarming words from your Highest Self. Honor and accept that you are fabulous.

If you feel lack, you will experience lack. If you feel love, you will experience love. That's why we've been working on our internal dialogue to get rid of the nastiest parts of the inner critic and bring in positive feelings—because feelings are the key. You can say "I am beautiful" over and over, much like a mantra, but unless you honestly feel, deep down in your bones, that you are beautiful, you are transmitting conflicting messages. One message is your thought form "I am beautiful," and the other message is your feeling of not being beautiful. This feeling message of being in lack is canceling out the positive message. In fact, the feeling is much more powerful than the thinking. The best beauty secret of all time is this: When you feel beautiful, you send out beautiful energy, and people react to that by seeing you as beautiful. They compliment you on how lovely you look, and you radiate beauty. The circle is complete. It's that simple.

### EXERCISE 3.2: MIRROR EXERCISE

Here's an exercise to test whether you have fully incorporated your list of positive reinforcers or whether you may want to tap or blow up some more roses.

1. Take out your list of heart traits from the previous exercise.

2. Stand in front of a mirror and read your list aloud. Read it slowly and deliberately. Notice any sensations that come up from your body as you read your list of attributes. Take notes about where the sensations are coming from (stomach, heart, throat, back) and any memories that pop into your mind as you say each word. You may feel silly standing there reading a list of positive attributes, but this is truly a powerful lesson.

3. If you feel resistance in your body to any of your attributes, then do some more tapping on that issue or blow up a rose. Send those feelings down your grounding cord. Sweep them out of your aura. You are getting to the root of your belief system and uncovering areas of lack instead of acceptance.

4. Breathe deeply, laugh at your self-consciousness, and enjoy the experience.

When you're living a life of purpose, you're living a life of joy. You're content, happy, and fulfilled because you know you're doing, being, and having exactly what is right for you. In the mirror exercise, you might have uncovered some thoughts and feelings that were outside of the feeling of joy.

You might have experienced feelings of unworthiness or lack concerning how you are currently living your life. Perhaps you heard your inner voice saying, "One of my heart traits can't be kindness to others because of what I said to so-and-so yesterday." If you were outside of joy at that moment, breathe.

As you come to accept your heart traits at a deep cellular level, your Spirit, your Highest and Best Self, will consciously remind you of where you're out of integrity—or not aligned—with a heart trait. Don't beat yourself up; just accept it with humor and acknowledge that you have work to do. We all have work to do. We don't ridicule a baby as she is learning to walk. We give her love and encouragement as she learns to take her first steps. You are that baby, so be kind to yourself. Pat yourself on the back. Validate and honor every one of your baby steps. Accept that you are learning a new way of living and that it will take time to get over the awkwardness. Remind yourself that every time you bring your experiences into alignment with your Spirit, you are moving one step closer to living your life on purpose—a life of joy.

## Walking Your Talk

Your next step is to identify one specific example of how you are currently out of alignment with one of your heart traits. Your job is to take action and correct the situation. Go easy and choose something that is attainable. For example, if one of your heart traits is courage, but you have avoided having a difficult conversation with a coworker because you're afraid of what might come of it, go ahead and have that conversation. Rehearse it ahead of time, and feel compassion and love as you speak, but clear the issue. Have the courage to go forth and conquer the situation. Afterward, please set aside some time to validate your action and honor yourself for correcting an out-of-alignment situation.

You may have thought of some more out-of-alignment issues. The next step is to take care of them. The following exercise outlines a way to set up an action plan, allowing you to walk your talk and live your life on purpose.

---

### EXERCISE 3.3: COMING INTO ALIGNMENT

1. In your journal, list your first heart trait from exercise 3.1. Skip down about five or six lines and list your second heart trait. Keep going, skipping about five or six lines between each heart trait until you have them all listed.

2. Now sit in silence for a moment. Breathe; become still and feel your body quiet. Ask that any information come to you about where you might be out of alignment with your first heart trait.

3. Under your first heart trait, immediately begin writing any situations that come to mind. Don't worry, you won't have to share this list with anyone. So be honest. You know in your heart whether you are in or out of alignment. Keep going through your list of heart traits until you have touched on each one.

4. In some areas, you may find that you're totally in alignment with your heart trait. Congratulate

yourself. Write down a couple of positive comments about the joy you feel right now.

5. For those heart traits where you need to realign, first make sure that the voice you heard is your own. If the voice isn't yours, then blow up a rose to move that negative voice out of your system. If the voice is yours, then come up with a plan of action—something you could do to rectify the situation. It does not need to be audacious. In fact, please make it doable. As an example, let's say that one of your heart traits is honesty. You feel good that you act in an honest way most of the time. Yet you also know that when it comes to filling out your income tax return, you are not completely honest. Don't beat yourself up, but do set up an action plan to remedy the situation. Maybe you've been overly liberal in the way you've written off certain expenses, labeling them "business" when in reality they're personal.

6. Commit to rectifying the situation. Write down the steps you're willing to take and the time period in which you're committing to accomplish this task. Know that you are making a commitment to correct the situation and then walk a new path in the future. Give yourself a gold star for being truthful about your lack of honesty and move on to your next trait.

7. After you have looked at each trait and made your list of items that need correction, make a to-do list for this week and the coming weeks and months.

8. As you come out of meditation, commit to completing your to-do list within a reasonable time frame.

Then commit to doing things differently from now on. Remember that being in alignment with your heart traits brings you joy, contentment, peace, and happiness. You are walking your talk and living a life full of integrity and joy. Congratulations!

## Create Your Statement of Being: Your Life's Intention

Journalist Clare Boothe Luce reportedly asked John F. Kennedy, "A great man is one sentence. Abraham Lincoln's was 'He preserved the Union and freed the slaves.' What's yours?"

You have a descriptive sentence too. In fact, I like to think in terms of a full paragraph, because life is too robust to capture it all in one phrase. You have already done all the legwork, so now you just need to put pen to paper.

Return to your heart traits list. We are going to fashion that list into a statement of being. Personally, I don't make New Year's resolutions. Instead, I re-create my statement of being every year on New Year's Day. I have found that most people state their New Year's resolutions in a negative form. Maybe that's why most resolutions never come to pass.

So come from the positive, from a position of feeling your emotion instead of a should. For example, when forming a resolution you might say to yourself, "Yuck, I don't like my body. I need to lose weight. My New Year's resolution is to drop fifteen pounds by March." Notice how that is a negative statement. You are in a state of resistance to your current weight and therefore are not accepting your present-moment body. You might not be the ideal weight for your body frame, but until you can accept all of you, including that roly-poly tummy or those large thighs, you will be in a state of resistance, a state of lack.

In addition, whatever you believe about yourself is reflected back to you and becomes your reality. If you are ashamed of your body, you will attract those same frequencies—shame and invalidation—back to you. It's as if a giant magnet is inside your space, attracting events and circumstances that are in direct correlation to your thoughts and feelings. Whether you experience love, fear, anger, happiness, or joy, what you think and feel you will be.

I don't think in terms of lack or resolutions. Instead, I choose terms more reflective of who I am in this present moment. My current statement of being goes something like this:

*I consciously create my reality every day with my thoughts and feelings. Therefore, each day I am grateful for all that life brings my way. I live in a state of appreciation for all that I have. I am happy, content, excited, joyful, kind, and generous. I give freely because I know there is more than enough for all of us. I love deeply and listen intently. I am present in the here and now. I live in a state of gratitude and peace, knowing that these feelings of goodwill and kindness are mirrored back to me in awe-filled ways that I cannot even imagine right now. I am open and ready to receive. I can have all of this and MORE.*

Notice how my statement of being is all about my thoughts and feelings. It's really a paragraph listing my heart traits in a little bit more detail. Most people believe that action is the most important part of creating the world they desire. They are all about do-ing: being active in making the life they want. People work hard and struggle through their daily tasks, believing that by physically doing something, they will attain what they desire. They have it backwards; it is really more important to think and feel it into being.

Remember, you really are the creator of your own reality. Everything that is coming to you is a direct result of your thoughts, feelings, and internal dialogue. You can be happy or sad, angry or not angry. You get to choose. Every minute is a new opportunity to determine your own reality. Change your thoughts and feelings and watch what happens to your reality.

---

### EXERCISE 3.4: WRITE YOUR STATEMENT OF BEING

1. Take out your name web and your list of heart traits.

2. Spend a moment reviewing your name web, specifically noticing all the positive statements that represent parts of your core personality.

3. Sit in silence for a moment and reflect upon the progress you have made so far in this journey toward understanding your inner dialogue. You have released some stories that are no longer true for you. You may have even come to terms with some of the angrier parts of that voice in your head, taming certain aspects of your inner critic.

4. Look over your list of heart traits and know that these traits are true representations of you, of your Highest and Best Self.

5. Reflect upon the qualities that represent your uniqueness, your gifts to the world. Come from a positive space. Be aware that every person, deep down at their core, has a special gift to share with the world.

6. Close your eyes and feel deep into your heart space. Consider the qualities, the energies, that are swirling around in your heart.

7. Maybe you are sensing the quality of kindness, creativity, or joy and lightheartedness. Craft those thoughts and feelings into a statement of being that reflects who you really are in this present moment. As you're writing, use the present tense and truly own the qualities that make you unique and special.

8. Read your statement of being aloud as you feel it resonate in truth throughout your body and your aura. Yes, this is truly who you really are.

We will use this statement of being throughout the rest of our journey together, so become comfortable with it, tweak it as you wish, and make it something you are truly proud to own.

### Energy Pointers

- How do you envision the space in the center of your head? Changing the details may make you feel more at home. You might choose to sit on a meditation cushion in the middle of a tropical rain forest or next to a waterfall of fanciful colors. You get to choose. Make the space your own.

- Send some healing energy down your grounding cord to the center of the earth. Acknowledge and be grateful for the nourishment you receive from the earth.

## Helpful Hints

- Energy isn't fussy. There isn't a right way or a wrong way of releasing energy, just your way. Relax. You're doing it right—I promise!

- The next time you look at your reflection in a mirror, smile and choose to see your beauty, not your flaws. Remember, what you think and feel you will be!

## Chapter 4

# Your Tree of Life

Imagine a tree, tall and massive, with branches full of fruit. Maybe it is an apple tree, a peach tree, or even an apricot tree. The roots of this tree run deep, all the way down to the center of the earth. They form a connection to Mother Earth, to all that has come before.

You are this tree.

The roots offer you strength and security, yet they are full of past generational issues and assumptions about who you truly are and your place in this world. So far in this book, you have worked to clear away some of the harmful growth on these roots—the negative self-talk that attacks, like a fungus or parasite, the very essence of you.

The trunk of this tree is massive. It gracefully bends in the winds of emotional strife and physical burden. It remains steady but pliant as it weathers the droughts of self-hate and the torrential rains of emotional outbursts. This is who you truly are, your essence, your soul. Each person's trunk is unique, an individual expression of the Divine. You have named your trunk through composing your statement of being.

The branches on your tree of life are many. They represent the paths you have walked, the opportunities you have encountered, and the choices you have made. Some branches are strong and true. Pruning others will make way for healthy new growth. There are branches that represent your job, your family and important relationships, your health, and many other parts of your life.

Pruning these branches is the simplification process you will undertake next on this journey of discovery. You will identify those paths that are in alignment with your essence and trim away those that prevent future growth. You will watch for branches with an overabundance of fruit—too many choices. You will use your list of heart traits and your statement of being as the yardstick against which all the current branches on your tree will be measured. From there you will validate those that are in alignment with your internal truth and prune those that are not. In the future, there will be no stray branches on this tree—only the strong, beautifully shaped ones that add to your tree's symmetry and grace.

---

### EXERCISE 4.1: DRAW YOUR OWN TREE OF LIFE

The tree of life is a metaphor intended to help clarify how our day-to-day activities impact our ability to live a life full of purpose and meaning. As we tame our inner critic, we begin to hear the whispers of our Spirit calling us to follow our true path. The purpose of this exercise is to visually remind us where we are in alignment with our true essence and where we are not.

1. Draw your own tree of life, labeling each part of the tree. The trunk represents your soul essence, your statement of being. Label your branches with all the various parts of your life. You may have branches named "My Health," "My Job," "My Outside Activities," "My Family and Friends," "The City Where I Live," etc.

2. Add pieces of fruit to your tree that represent the choices you face. If you're debating whether to eat less sugar or begin an exercise program, those choices would hang from the branch labeled "My Health."

3. Below your tree, write out your statement of being. Now you're ready to examine the various branches in more detail.

**Branch #1: My Health**

1. Look at the "My Health" branch of your tree and compare it to your statement of being. Consider all the components: your physical health and your emotional well-being. Read your statement of being and reflect upon how it aligns with the state of your health. Maybe one of the words on your statement of being is "kindness." Ask yourself whether you are being kind to your body or pushing it too hard. Maybe you are making excuses for not going to the gym, or maybe you choose to exercise even when your body is in pain.

2. Write out a plan of action, listing ways to be kind to your body. You might opt to eat one vegetarian dinner a week or sign up for that dance class after all. The choice is up to you. Now go a little bit deeper. If one of your heart traits is "compassion," evaluate whether you show compassion to those who do *not* take care of their bodies. You may be full of judgment and criticism toward people who eat at fast-food restaurants or are overweight. Remember that your thoughts and feelings are powerful. What energy surrounds you when it comes to the topic of your health?

### Branch #2: My Job

1. Next, consider the branch called "My Job." Spend a moment writing down the main activities at your place of employment. For example, let's say you're in charge of a major update to the company's strategic plan. It takes up about 30 percent of your time each and every day. You talk about your work with family members when you get home at night, and you discuss it with friends on the weekends.

2. Look over your statement of being and your list of heart traits to see if this project is an outward expression of some of the qualities that are true expressions of who you really are.

3. Now look at another primary work activity. It could be that this task takes up another large block of your time, but it's filled with routine tasks. While your strategic-planning activity fills you with excitement,

this particular activity is boring and not exciting. Envision a way to tip the scales. There may be a part of the routine work that could be shifted to someone else or given up altogether. Just because it's been done one way for years doesn't mean that's the best way. Think of how you might free up some of your time each day to add another small project that is in alignment with who you really are. You make choices every minute of every day. Maybe there is a choice you can make that will tip the workload to be more in alignment with your heart traits.

4. On the other end, maybe your job requires you to work alone and under the direct supervision of your boss, with little room for individual expression of ideas. The income from this job may be essential to your family, but the job itself does not nourish the core of your being. Although it may not be possible to prune this branch just yet, begin to imagine a job that would feed your soul. Spend some time paying close attention to what excites you, touches you, inspires you to think in a completely new way, or even frustrates you. Ask your closest friends for help. Have them list all the jobs and occupations that they believe would bring you joy. Sometimes those closest to us can see the entire forest and not just one tree close up, as we might. You may come up with a plan to go back to school at night or to volunteer on the weekends to fuel your passion. Or you may conclude that while your current job does not align well with your heart traits, it does provide you with a great

income, allowing you to spend your leisure time as you choose. That may be exactly the right fit for you. There is not a right or wrong answer here. The task is to become aware of the choices you are making.

5. Spend some time in quiet reflection and meditation, checking in with the other branches on your tree. Check them all against your statement of being.

6. Be clear about what is working in your life and what is not. Make a list of what you are willing to change during the next few months, and then follow through on making those changes. This is a process. Change won't happen overnight, but as you realign the parts of your life that are not working, you are making room for new, exciting opportunities to come your way. It is all up to you.

**Branch #3: My Outside Activities**

1. Look at the branch called "Outside Activities." Make a quick list of all the activities you are currently involved in outside of your job. Maybe you are taking a yoga class on Monday nights and you drive your son to his soccer games on Saturdays. Look at your daily planner for the past month. Book club, the online course you are taking, carpool commitments: write them all down.

2. Now put that list side by side with your statement of being. Look for areas of correlation. Circle those activities. Affirm that they offer you sustenance and nourishment.

3. Now look at the other items, the ones that are not circled. Ask yourself whether you took on these activities as shoulds. Do you frantically race to the yoga class every week just because you paid for it? Do you stop for fast food because you're rushing to get the kids home after soccer practice? Don't allow yourself to dwell in the energy of judgment. This is an exercise in pruning the not-so-helpful items to make room for new growth. If you are so busy that you cannot find room for a new activity that you know would bring you joy, then it really is time to let something go. Decide what you're going to prune to make way for the yet-to-be-discovered ways of being that are in alignment with your essence. Write it down and commit to taking action within the coming week.

4. Maybe you decide that you really want to continue with the yoga class, but your son's out-of-town soccer game this weekend is something you will pass up. Yes, it sounds crazy to take time for yourself instead of attending an activity of your child. However, reflect upon what nourishes you the most. You cannot do everything, and we often sacrifice our own pleasures to take care of the people we love. Remember, as any flight attendant will tell you, put on your own oxygen mask first. Maybe that yoga class is just that: your oxygen. Think deeply and validate your own worthiness.

## The Art of Saying No

As you may have realized from doing the previous exercise, if you are to prune any branches from your tree of life, you need to learn the art of saying no. And yes, saying no is an art! It's all about coming from your own heart, not leaking your energy out to others in shoulds and must-dos.

Defining your path with clarity, as you have done, makes it easier to say no, because you can define what is in alignment with your inner knowingness. However, for most of us, this is still a difficult assignment. Practicing in front of a mirror might make it easier. Say to yourself, "You know I'd love to help out with this project, but I just can't. I'm way overbooked," or "Gee, I'm so sorry, but I can't take that on right now." Period. End of sentence. You do not need to justify why you can't, you just need to say no. Leave no doubt, no room for maneuvering. You want to be clear in your no while coming from a place of compassion and honesty.

Removing the energy blocks from your voice and throat will help too. As you say "no," imagine the words flowing out of your throat in crystal-clear color, surrounded by warmth, honesty, and clarity. Saying no with clarity and gentleness allows you to stand in your own power.

Practice saying no. Write about your experiences. Validate your clarity, your strength, and the compassion you hold for yourself. Then check in with the branches on your tree—the ones you have pruned that are now lying on the ground in front of you. Remember that if your no is not crystal clear, those branches will magically reattach to your tree! They will jump right up off the grass and reattach to the trunk, and you will find yourself right back where you started a few weeks ago: overwhelmed and frustrated. Prune with clarity and finality. Make your no stick. Make it permanent. Make it definitive. Come from your heart and mean it. No going back.

A well-known proverb says, "All the flowers of all the tomorrows are in the seeds of today." Pruning the branches of your tree will result in new growth, new ways of being, new opportunities to be more of who you were meant to be. Pruning the branches that are not in alignment with your essence will allow your other branches to bear fruit and then seeds: the next generation of new ideas.

So cut back those branches. Make room for the new. Practice saying no. Practice standing in your own power and not leaking it to someone else. Know that as you prune back to the essentials—to the activities that are in alignment with your internal wisdom—you will blossom. Make room in your life for *you*.

As with any difficult assignment, validate your progress. Gather up the branches that do not work and dispose of them. Make a list of all those shoulds that you are ready to let go of. Write them all down. Look at this list as you plan your calendar for the next few weeks. Rejoice in your ability to set your own agenda.

## The Dog Poops of Life

Now that your pruning is complete and your tree is a fair representation of who you really are, there is one more thing to consider: the dog poops of life. Let's talk about what happens to your plan, your life, when the unexpected happens—when the poop hits the fan, so to speak. When your plans go awry, when the car runs out of gas, when the baby is crying and you have to get to a meeting.

Humor is a great tool to help us move from resistance to appreciation. This is not the laughing "ha-ha" type of humor. This is about stepping back and looking at ourselves with detachment, neutrality, and amusement. In this space of detachment, we are able to gain a little distance from our emotions. We are able to discern the difference between our true state of being and a piece of foreign energy stuck in our space.

Neutrality allows us to ask, to wonder why, and to move into a state of acceptance of things just the way they are, without drama. When the car runs out of gas and the baby is crying, when the events in our lives are chaotic and discordant, we can either match that vibration and become stressed over the situation, or we can shift our perspective to one of acceptance, neutrality, and amusement. In that state we are no longer focused on what we don't want—in this case, the crazy antics of our day. We have moved from a grumbling state of mind, which has a lower energetic vibration, to the higher-vibrational frequency of allowance and appreciation. We have removed ourselves from the drama, and through humor, we can stand back and look at the current circumstances in a completely new light.

It could be that the crying baby is letting us know that we are not grounded and that we may be allowing other people's energies to enter our space. It could be that we've taken on too many obligations and shoulds from other people and haven't had time to notice that the car is low on gas. Standing back from the situation and looking at it with neutrality and awareness has a huge impact on the quality of our experience.

Everything within our universe breaks down into its purest form as a vibrating mass of atoms and subatomic particles. This oscillating energy doesn't stay in one place, it vibrates, sending out shockwaves of particles—pieces of itself—into space. Everything in its purest form is a block of energy that resonates and vibrates. Our thoughts, feelings, and emotions are part of this everything, so they, too, vibrate and send waves of energy out into the cosmos.

No thought is ever lost. The crying baby may be picking up some of our anger, resentment, or frustration. But if we settle ourselves down by centering and grounding to the earth, the baby may tune in to our vibrations and stop fussing. Grounding will not fill up our empty gas tank, but it will allow us to take a breath and see the situation from a different perspective.

Oprah said it best in the final episode of *The Oprah Winfrey Show*: "You are responsible for the energy that you create for yourself, and you're responsible for the energy that you bring to others. Please take responsibility for the energy you bring into this space."

The events, situations, and circumstances in your life are a direct result of your thoughts, feelings, and emotions—your magnetic pull, so to speak. And you can be responsible for those thoughts and feelings.

If you are in a state of gratitude and can accept the things that are—even the dog poops of life—you attract more harmony into your life. The result is happiness. You are in harmony, at peace, and in a state of acceptance with what is, and so you draw more harmony, peace, and acceptance into your life. Try it the next time you start to grumble about something. Add some amusement to the situation and see if your perspective shifts.

## Moving Through Resistance

Let's set the stage to reinforce all the positive changes in our lives. We all know how easy it is to slip back into old habits. It's hard to sustain a change, any change. Therefore, here are some suggestions on how to make new behaviors stick.

Anytime we move from where we are to where we want to be, we feel resistance. It is almost as if the status quo has a magnetic force of its own. If this force is stronger than our desire to make a change, we fall back into alignment with where we were before—and all our hard work, all our new ways, are forgotten. We return to the womb of comfort and security and rationalize away our attempted growth.

You don't want that to happen. You have come too far and learned too many interesting things to go back to where you started. Anytime you get that nagging feeling that a new behavior is too much, too difficult, too unsettling, ask yourself whose voice is in your head. It could be your mother's voice or your partner's voice. Once you have named that voice, use your tools to remove that energy from your space. Tap on the story, or put the voice in a rose and blow up the rose. Say to that voice, "Oh, I know you. You are the voice trying to keep me small. I think I've outgrown the need for your protection now, so please leave me alone." If you feel resistance in your space, sit with that resistance in meditation. Ask it to tell you its name and why it is in your life. You might be surprised by what you hear.

Let's take a look at the energy of resistance. In the next exercise, I suggest a way to visualize your feelings as colors and how to retain the colors that represent your best self while allowing colors that don't support you to drain away.

---

### EXERCISE 4.2: USING COLORFUL SOAP BUBBLES TO MOVE PAST RESISTANCE

Think back to one of the pruned branches from your tree of life. See the branch lying on the ground and feel how it wants to reattach—how the old way of being is trying to sneak back into your life. Maybe you said no to attending your son's out-of-town soccer game yesterday, but today you are about to pick up the phone and change your no to a yes. Or maybe you thought you were committed to making a change at work, but now you've hit an obstacle and your enthusiasm is waning. Whatever situation you find yourself in, it's possible to use your intuition to remove any energy blocks that are preventing you from living your life your way. Let's remove that resistance so you can stay on the path you've chosen.

1. Sit in silence, with your eyes closed. Be in the center of your head. (If you need to review this, see Exercise 1.5: Grounding Meditation.) Allow yourself a moment to settle. Ground yourself to the center of the earth. Become relaxed and comfortable, and take a couple of deep breaths. On each inhale, feel more of your own energy coming into the center of your

head. On each exhale, feel the stresses of the day, the foreign energy, leave your body and travel back down to the earth. Sink a little deeper in your chair as you come into alignment with the in-and-out motion of centering and grounding.

2. Now think of the change you would like to make and the resistance you feel to making that change permanent.

3. Imagine a soap bubble forming in front of your closed eyes. Ask this soap bubble to fill with the colors representing the change you would like to make permanent. For example, let's assume that you have decided to take an art class on Tuesday nights as a way to express one of your heart traits. This art class is in alignment with your statement of being, and you were really jazzed about finding an activity that's just for you. Yet now, in the third week of the class, you've hit the wall of resistance. Your enthusiasm is waning, and all of your good intentions are about to go out the door. Before you quit your art class, look at the energy of the situation.

4. As you sit in meditation, imagine the bubble representing your art class in front of you. See it filled with color. If you cannot see it clearly, don't worry; just imagine what it would be like if you could see it. Relax and allow your imagination to flow. You might have a sense of just knowing or imagining colors. Relax and go with it.

5. Think about what those colors mean to you. See if they're flowing or static, angry or calm. Each person

interprets colors in a different way. There is no right or wrong answer, just your answer. When I look at my soap bubbles, an orange-red is anger and a blue-green is calm. Buttercup yellow is joy and dusty purple is sorrow. Black tar represents resistance, as in "What can't I accept?" A milky, cloudy white is unconsciousness, as in "What can't I see?" And my all-time favorite is a deep pink-red. That's my perfectionism showing.

6. Go within, look at your soap bubble, and begin to understand your world. Let's say that as you bring the bubble representing your art class into focus, you notice that it is filled with a mixture of dark blue and chaotic-looking gray. There is a big streak of dark pink over on the right side and some fairly see-through buttercup yellow on the left side. You might ask yourself what all of this means; thoughts might float through your mind. Don't discount those thoughts. They are real. Maybe the dark blue represents seriousness to you, and the chaotic gray symbolizes being overwhelmed by trying hard to master a new skill. The buttercup yellow may represent joy, letting you know that deep down this art class is in alignment with your Spirit. As you come to understand the energy surrounding your situation, decide if you'd like to change its vibration.

7. If you've found some energies that you are ready to change, put a grounding cord on your bubble. Imagine a large, hollow tube with one end attached to the bubble and other end attached to the center of

the earth. Allow this grounding cord to drain out all the dark, not-you colors from your bubble. Watch as seriousness, effort, chaos, and perfectionism flow down the grounding cord and leave your bubble. Once your project bubble is drained of all those dark, hard-to-see-through colors, fill it with more light and playful colors. No one says we have to be serious and effortful all the time. Lighten up! Watch your bubble fill in with your chosen colors, and feel the calmness spread into your body and mind. Remove the grounding cord and allow the bubble to float off into the ether.

8. You've changed the dynamics of your situation by changing its energetic vibration. Instead of thoughts of seriousness and perfectionism, you are filled with creativity and focus. Sit in that calm, clear state for a moment or two, and then come out of meditation. Anytime you find yourself fighting with the energy of resistance, step into meditation and examine that energy. This is using your intuition to remove any resistance to moving into new states of being. Congratulate yourself. You've just learned a really cool way to remove the blocks to living life the way you want to: full of purpose and meaning.

## Dreaming Big

The first step to taming your inner critic and living a life on purpose is consciously observing your current state of being. You have done that by drawing your tree of life and reviewing branches on your tree. The next step is pruning those parts of your life that are not in alignment with Spirit; learning to say no to those activities not in alignment with your own true path. You have done that too. Lastly, to help you move beyond the pull of the status quo, you have learned to consciously shift the vibrational frequency of your thoughts and feelings by reading and altering its energetic signature. Now it's time to start the dreaming, the contemplating of what your life would look like if you brought all areas of your life into alignment with your statement of being.

In her book *Something More: Excavating Your Authentic Self,* Sarah Ban Breathnach shares a creative approach to creating a life in alignment with Spirit. She suggests searching through magazines and catalogues for images that represent parts of the life you would like to create, and storing the images in nine-by-twelve-inch manila envelopes. Each envelope can be the focus of one life area. Breathnach recommends adding an extra envelope labeled "Mystery" for images that don't fit neatly into a category. Let's use this approach as a jumping-off point to creating a life on purpose.

---

**EXERCISE 4.3: PICTURING YOUR DREAM LIFE**

1. Gather enough manila envelopes to represent the main branches on your tree of life and enough extra envelopes to represent various aspects of your statement of being.

2. Label some of the envelopes with words representing the branches on your tree of life. Go big! As an example, you might write "My Ideal Job" or "My Ultimate Vacation."

3. Label the remaining manila envelopes with descriptive words from your statement of being. Use feeling-state words such as "kindness," "joy," or "empathy." You may have ten or twelve envelopes, representing both the concrete parts of your life, such as your health and your job, and the feeling states of your soul, such as kindness and joy.

4. Over the next few weeks, as you come across visual images representing your desired outcomes, cut them out of magazines or copy them from pages on social media sites. Add these images to your manila envelopes. When you come across a quote or an image that warms your heart for no apparent reason, save it in one of your envelopes. You may choose to do your own artwork representing the events, circumstances, and feeling states that you would like to permeate your life. This is your dreaming stage, so have some fun and put all thoughts of logic and reason aside.

5. In the last chapter, you will open the envelopes and use your saved images as a jumping-off point to designing a life full of purpose and meaning. But for now, just clip images and words that attract you, toss them in the appropriate envelopes, and forget about them. If you peek in the envelopes too often, you're likely to invalidate some of your choices, so just cut, snip, and save for now.

Consider all that you have accomplished in this chapter. Think about how differently you see yourself, how differently you speak about yourself and others. Spend some time in quiet contemplation. Be grateful and write about how you have already changed from the time you started reading this book and working on the exercises.

## Energy Pointers

- What color signifies the energy of peace to you? What do you feel is the color of the energy of perfectionism? Begin to build your own library of color-emotion associations.

- Spend some time appreciating the small wonders in your life. Find three things to be grateful for each day.

- You'll be very happy at the end of this book if you've done Exercise 4.3: Picturing Your Dream Life. If you skipped it, go back and dream big. You'll thank me later.

## Helpful Hints

- Saying no with a smile is a great way of making sure trimmed branches (representing activities that don't serve you or align with your statement of being) don't reattach to your tree of life.

- What you think and feel you will be. Test out that statement for yourself.

## Chapter 5

# Chakras and Your Life Force

Within your physical body there is an energetic body, which you've been working with quite a lot already. As your grounding cord drains foreign energy from your system or you blow up a rose, you are releasing energy that has been stored in your aura and *chakras*. Chakras are wheels of spinning energy located along the central axis of your body that house the energy of your thoughts and feelings (see figure 3). These bands of vibrating energy literally connect your aura to your physical form. They provide information to your endocrine system, regulating your hormones and balancing the energy within your body.

The ancients were well aware of the chakra system and wrote about life force flowing throughout the body. (In Chinese medicine, life force is called *chi*; in Sanskrit, it is *prana*.) Western medicine is slowly coming to grips with the idea that energy flows through the body and affects our emotions and physical health.

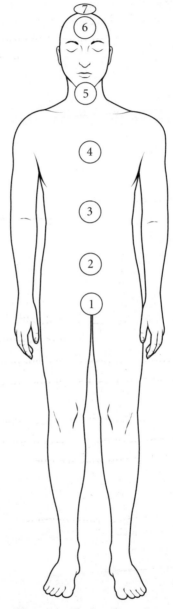

*Figure 3: Chakra Locations*

I think of chakras as energetic way stations linking our Spirit to our physical body. When a person's chakra is full of foreign energy, the natural flow of life force is constricted and may, over time, cause dis-ease in the body (and the soul). When we change the way we hold this tension—say we blow up a rose or tap out a story—we release this tension, which affects our physical body's state of ease. As our body and its energetic system come into balance, we create better health. Our thoughts and feelings truly do affect our physical body.

The Internet is full of all kinds of information about chakras and auras. Some of that information is in alignment with the way I see energies and some of it is not. Neither is right or wrong. Remember the story about the blindfolded men describing an elephant? One man stood at the trunk, and because he was only in touch with that one part of the whole, his description varied dramatically from the other blindfolded man who was touching the elephant's tail. Both men were processing their own reality, but neither had access to the whole. In other words, I see it one way, and you see it another way.

It is the same with chakras. I may see a chakra as a multi-colored, vibrating mass of energy. When you close your eyes and visualize a chakra, you may see one or two colors moving in a dance of oscillating waves. We both must stand in our own truth. Some texts present each chakra as a set color: the first chakra is red, the second chakra is orange, and so on. Some say that the third chakra, which is located around the navel, is our power center, while others say our power comes from our second chakra, believed to be at the sacrum.

You will need to process this information, take what fits for you, and adapt my suggestions to find what resonates as your own truth. I see energies as floating among the different chakras, reflecting our changing thoughts and moods. For instance, the energy in the third chakra, your power center, might be leaking into the second chakra, your emotional center, causing you to see your power in your second chakra. Or, as you view your third-chakra energy, you might see someone else's second-chakra emotional energy distorting your view. What you see is what you see. Stand in your own truth, at all times.

## The First Chakra

The first chakra is located at the base of the spine and runs from the front of the body to the back of the body. This swirling disk of energy is concerned with our body's survival: having enough food, water, and shelter.

The energy of family and friends is a frequent occupant of this chakra. You may hear your mother's voice encouraging you to finish everything on your plate every time you sit down at the dinner table. Or you may hear your old football coach telling you to buck up and play through your pain. Or perhaps you sense your father's energy letting you know that the new home you just purchased is a little too big, a little too grand. Using a grounding cord to remove all this foreign energy from your space is a powerful way to reclaim it as your own.

The adrenal glands are associated with the first chakra, and they send out hormones to alert the body to a potentially dangerous situation. You may feel the area around the base of your spine flare up when you are under stress or when you remember a dramatic event from your past.

## The Second Chakra

The second chakra is called the sacral chakra. It is located about two inches below the belly button and, like all the chakras, runs from the front to the back of the body. I see this as the chakra of emotions and sexual energy.

A healthy second chakra vibrates in a state of permission to have whatever emotion we are experiencing in the moment and to express that emotion appropriately. In other words, we are able to cry when we feel the need to cry and to be angry when we need to be angry. We remain in control of our emotions, yet at the same time we can express them fully and appropriately.

If this chakra is full of shoulds, then you could be limiting the range of emotions you can comfortably express. You may feel it's inappropriate to show anger under any circumstances, or perhaps you're unable to show your vulnerable side. If there is foreign energy in this chakra, you may find yourself running other people's emotions instead of your own. For instance, if your friend is a drama queen and you have taken on her emotions, you may find yourself playing the victim to your circumstances instead of constructively dealing with your problems.

Uncovering your true path is a tough assignment if this chakra is filled with outside influences. Discovering the real you, your Highest and Best Self, is a process of removing the layers of other people's thoughts, other people's emotions, and other people's shoulds from your space. The next time you are experiencing an intense emotion such as anger or frustration, pause and feel the energy stirring in the sacral chakra. Use your awareness to determine whether this is truly your emotion or someone else's stuck in your second chakra.

## The Third Chakra

This chakra is located in the abdomen, close to the belly button. It is our power center. A healthy third chakra has just the right amount of energy necessary to fuel the body. We can turn our power down when we are resting and then amp it up when we are running errands. Foreign energy that may lodge in this chakra causes a person's power to run either too high or too low for the present circumstances. An example is a person who gets hyper-excited and then cannot fall asleep at night. Foreign energy in the third chakra might come from a person who is trying to live their life vicariously through you. Or, if you are a control freak, know that as you try to control every detail of your project, you are spewing your energy in all directions, leaving very little to fuel your own body.

My favorite energy to look at in the third chakra is perfectionism. Those of us who cannot let go of the need to be perfect probably have lots of someone else's energy in this space. Often your mother's energy is there, reminding you to wear a coat, comb your hair, stand up straight, or smile more often.

Check to see whose voice is in your third chakra. Use some of your tools, such as blowing up a rose, to remove that foreign energy. Add some confidence and vitality to this space. Determine to set your own internal agenda and not be governed by your inner critic and the voice of should.

## The Fourth Chakra

Located at the heart center—the middle of your chest at the level of your heart—the fourth chakra is what I call your affinity space, the seat of self-worth. We have already used some exercises to clear out some of the foreign energy in this space: those self-deprecating thoughts, those feelings of inadequacy and invalidation. Your personal magnet is located in this chakra, calling to you events and circumstances that are in alignment with how you see yourself. Check in with your fourth chakra. Are you better able to look in the mirror and appreciate the incredible being that you are?

Our work together is centered on the notion of bringing your chakras into alignment with who you really are. You will begin to hear the voice of your Spirit, your Highest and Best Self, instead of the voices of your family and peers. As we continue our work together, your fourth chakra will become brighter as you tame your inner critic.

Spend some time reading your statement of being. Know that you are here on Earth to bring forth your unique talents and gifts and share them with the world. Shine bright!

## The Fifth Chakra

The fifth chakra is located in the throat and is the seat of our ability to communicate, verbally and nonverbally. A healthy fifth chakra allows us to speak our truth and communicate our thoughts with ease and comfort. If this chakra is clogged with foreign energy, you may find it hard to express your thoughts clearly and fully.

The following throat-clearing exercise will allow you to clearly communicate your needs, speak your truth, and fully express your thoughts and feelings.

---

### EXERCISE 5.1: CLEARING YOUR THROAT ENERGY

To do this exercise, we will use the blowing-up-a-rose tool from chapter 2 (exercise 2.4). This is an easy and effective way to remove foreign energy from any one of your chakras.

1. Start by getting into a comfortable sitting position. Have your feet flat on the floor. Close your eyes, sit quietly, and notice your breath going in and out of your nose. Being fully aware of your breath, breathe slowly and steadily for a few minutes. Notice how you relax more and more with each breath.

2. Now bring your awareness to your throat. Notice whether your throat feels scratchy, tight, or sore. Maybe it feels as if you have something stuck in the back of your throat.

3. Imagine a rose floating in front of you. Put a giant magnet in this rose. Ask yourself whether there's something you have wanted to say to someone all your life, but you have never been able to find the right words. Maybe those words are stuck in the back of your throat, just itching to come out.

4. Relax your jaw and open your mouth wide, as if you were yawning. Imagine the words coming out of your mouth in a stream of colors.

5. Watch the colors as they leave your body and enter the rose. Notice what colors are streaming from your throat. Feel the emotions attached to the words that you have wanted to say. Ask those emotions to leave your body and enter the rose. With your mouth still open, expel the final stuck energies from your throat and watch as the rose fills up with the energies of what you could not say.

6. Breathe in through your nose and visualize your breath like the wind blowing out the last of the debris from the back of your throat, straight out through the front of your throat. See the magnet in the rose draw to it the remaining stuck energy.

7. Now blow up the rose and watch as all that energy disappears into the ether. Feel yourself relaxed and at peace.

8. Now open your eyes and take a deep breath. Come out of meditation when you are ready.

## The Sixth Chakra

Often called the third eye, the sixth chakra is located right above and between the eyebrows. From here we intuitively see the world around us. If our sixth chakra is healthy and free of other people's energies, then we see the world as it is, without judgment. Opening up the sixth chakra and cleaning out all the thoughts and feelings of others allows us to see our world as it truly is, as we connect to our inner wisdom, our own truth.

Seeing the world through our third eye allows us to experience a sixth sense, a way of sensing the energies of the thoughts and feelings of the people in our lives. In most cases, young children have a wide-open sixth chakra. Over time, their parents and society in general may invalidate these sixth-sense experiences, causing a fog of uncertainty to descend over this energy center. But what can be shut can also be reopened!

We are literally clearing away the fog of invalidation and opening up to our clairvoyant abilities as we sit in the center of our heads and do some of the exercises in this book. When we picture a soap bubble out in front of us and imagine colors streaming into that bubble, we are using our intuition, our clairvoyance, to see with our sixth chakra.

## The Seventh Chakra

Unlike the other six chakras, the seventh chakra is not a wheel; it's a ring of energy, sitting almost like a monarch's crown, on top of the head. Not surprisingly, it is sometimes referred to as the crown chakra. This energy center is your connection to the Divine. However you see that Source of All, this is your space of communion. When the seventh chakra is vibrating in tune with the Divine, you are vibrating in a state of knowing your own Spirit.

If there is foreign energy in your seventh chakra, you may be uncomfortable presenting yourself fully to the world, hiding certain aspects of your personality from view.

The work we're doing together is about removing foreign energy from your seventh chakra, helping you to shine bright, to stand in your own truth, and to become comfortable in your own skin. Being seen for who you really are, and sharing your personal light with the world, is the focus of your journey of discovery.

## How the Endocrine System Works with the Chakras

The chakras and the physical body communicate through the endocrine, or glandular, system—which includes the adrenals, the reproductive glands, the pancreas, and others. Each gland produces hormones that act as chemical messengers that stimulate a physical response in the body.

When we hold tension or an emotion in a particular chakra, this tension is communicated to the body through the secretion of hormones. When the tension continues to be present over a period of time, we create a symptom on the physical level. Most of us know what heartache feels like. I believe that when we feel this ache in the center of our chest, we are acknowledging on an energetic level a constriction in our heart chakra. We feel the emotional upheaval of sadness, pain, and loss. Our heart center feels heavy and about to break. Our thoughts are full of what-ifs and why-did-this-have-to-happen? If we allow this emotional state to fester, we may develop dis-ease at the body level. In my personal experience, the pain lessens when I ground myself, consciously remove foreign energy from my space, and intend to fill myself in with self-affirming energies.

Our experience of being who we really truly are—the thoughts and feelings that resonate and vibrate within us—is called our *life force*. This life-force energy permeates our whole being, radiating from the chakras out to the physical body. By removing foreign energy from our chakras, we release tension in our body, allowing our life force—our chi—to move freely, bringing balance and harmony to mind, body, and soul. When we imagine popping a golden sun and feel that energy course through our body and aura, we are actually filling in with more of our own life-force energy.

## Earth and Cosmic Energies

As I mentioned in chapter 1, our grounding cord drains foreign and negative energies out of our system, returning them to Mother Earth. The golden sun tool helps us integrate, bringing our own our life force back into our body, fueling our passions, our dreams, and allowing us to manifest the life that we are meant to live.

Most people are using their spiritual energy, their life force, to keep their bodies running. It's difficult to fuel your dreams if your body is using most of your life energy just to get through your hectic day.

I would like to introduce you to two other energies: *earth energy* and *cosmic energy*. You may call upon these at any time to act as your body's fuel, allowing your life force to be your soul's fuel, thereby bringing your dreams and desires into reality.

Earth and cosmic energies are neutral—free of foreign energy—and are available to everyone in unlimited supply. When you introduce these two energies into your body, they will do the work of fueling your bodily systems, leaving your life force, your chi, free to fuel your passions, dreams, and manifestations.

Many cultures around the world draw upon the earth for nourishment and the heavens for inspiration. Follow along in meditation as I explain how to employ these two neutral energies.

---

### EXERCISE 5.2: MOTHER EARTH
### AND FATHER SKY MEDITATION

1. Sit in a comfortable chair, with your feet flat on the floor and your eyes closed.

2. Take a couple of deep breaths and move your awareness to the space in the center of your head. Be in your inner stillness, your special meditative place between your ears, behind your eyes, and in the seat of your intuition. Be there now.

3. From this space of internal awareness, look down at your grounding cord. If it looks tattered or worn, release it from around your hips and see it fall to the center of the earth. Now imagine a brand-new grounding cord. See it out in front of you, strong and wide. Visualize this grounding cord around your lower body. Feel it drop to the center of the earth and feel it sink into the core. Feel an upward tug, letting you know that your grounding cord is anchored securely into the center of the planet.

4. Now imagine your aura around you. Feel it emanating about eighteen inches out from your body and extending below your feet. Feel its ovoid shape and see it fused to your grounding cord, making an airtight seal. Feel your aura release into your grounding cord, and imagine that suction carrying

a wisp of someone else's thought back down to the center of the earth. Feel yourself sink into your chair just a little bit more.

5. Breathe. Feel relaxed and centered. You are grounded to the earth, sitting in your own aura, your own space. Claim the space from the outer edges of your aura all the way into the interior reaches of your body as your own. This is your space. You are the master of your own universe and you get to be in charge here. If you want to add a color to your aura, do so now. Maybe you want to be surrounded by pink, sky blue, or the color of joy. You decide.

6. Keeping your eyes closed, bring your attention to the soles of your feet. Intend for some earth energy to come up from the core of the planet and enter the soles of your feet. Visualize the earth energy entering your feet and moving up your legs, to your knees, and then up to your thighs. Feel the energy surge through your legs and enter the front of your first chakra right at the pubic mound. Feel the energy course through your first chakra and waterfall down the back of that chakra, into your grounding cord, returning to the center of the earth. Choose a color or vibration for your earth energy. Maybe you want to feel the energy of pink or dusty orange. Maybe lime-green earth energy is more in tune with your system right now. You get to choose.

7. Sit with this energy for a moment. Feel it coming up through your soles, your ankles, swooshing around in your knees, traveling up your thighs, and then

entering your first chakra. Feel it traveling through your first chakra and cascading out the back. This is a circuit of energy—coming up from the center of the earth, moving through the lower portion of your body, and then falling down your grounding cord to return to Mother Earth.

8. When this energy is running smoothly, you are ready to add some cosmic energy to the mix. Throughout history, we have turned our gaze to the heavens for inspiration. We reach for the stars and stretch our arms above our heads as we seek our connection to All That Is. Some call this "Father Sky energy," while others use the term "cosmic energy," "etheric energy," or "heavenly blessings." The name is not as important as the function. As humans, it's important to be connected to both the earth below us and the cosmos above us. We are spiritual beings residing in a physical body. By bringing in some cosmic energy, we are balancing our soul's yearning to be connected to All That Is with our physical body's desire to be rooted firmly in the earth.

9. Imagine reaching above your head and pulling down some cosmic energy, allowing it to enter your seventh chakra at the back of your head. This energy is lighter than the earth's energy, but it, too, is neutral and of unlimited supply. Think of a color that you would like to experience. Maybe you want to see what dusty-rose or sky-blue cosmic energy feels like. Maybe you feel adventurous and decide to pick a

translucent mixture of orange, green, and purple. Whatever color(s) you choose, intend for the cosmic energy to enter at the back of your crown chakra, travel down your neck, continue down your shoulders and back, and enter your first chakra at the base of your spine. Feel the energy give you a back massage as it travels from the top of your head and down your back to your first chakra.

10. Notice how both your earth and cosmic energies are mixing in your first chakra. The earth energy is coming in the front, and the cosmic energy is coming in from the back. The energies meet and mix together. This mixture travels out the front of the first chakra and up the front of your body. Feel it move up through your belly, your heart, your throat, your face. When it reaches your crown chakra, the mixture then shoots out of the top of your head, swirling down through your aura until it meets your grounding cord. Feel that energy as it makes the loop from the back of your head, down your spinal column, up your torso, out the top of your head.

11. Notice that some of the mixture has also flowed from your throat, down your arms, and out through your palms. The arm channels are your creative channels, and the energy that pulses like miniature whale spouts from your palms is your creative force.

12. Become aware of these energies as they run through your body. Imagine them fueling your body. Feel this energy as it revitalizes you. Bring your aware-

ness to being a part of the earth and a part of the cosmos. You are One With All, with your soul and body in balance and harmony, connected to Mother Earth and Father Sky.

13. Know that once you have turned this energy on, it will continue to run, supplying you with fresh fuel for the entire day.

14. Sit in this incredible energy field for another moment or two.

15. When you are ready, open your eyes, stand up, and stretch. Know that your grounding cord is still in place, that your aura bubble is still around you, and that your earth and cosmic energies are still running.

As you move earth and cosmic energy throughout your system, intend for it to clear the way so that your own thoughts and feelings, your life force, can infuse each of your chakras. Be balanced and in harmony with the heavens and the earth.

## Energy Pointers

- What color do you associate with the energy of self-worth? What's the color of the energy of effort? Continue to build your own library of associations.

- Add a new image to one of your manila envelopes that represents the word "comfort." Remember that we will be using Exercise 4.3: Picturing Your Dream Life in an upcoming chapter. If you skipped it, go back and dream big. You'll thank me later.

### Helpful Hints

- Your chakras are like apertures on a camera: they open and close depending upon the energy residing there. Consciously choose to open your sixth chakra (the third eye) a little wider.

- Being in effort keeps energy stuck where it is. Bring some lightness and amusement to your day. Intend for foreign energy to leave your system without a need to replay the event or circumstance. Keep the drama-queen energy at bay.

## Chapter 6

# The Energy of Relationships

In our society, we're taught to be empathetic. To come from someone else's perspective is to see the person and to empathize with them. Often we think that walking in another person's shoes, feeling someone else's pain, is a prerequisite to seeing the person for who they truly are. We call this having a relationship. When we're in a state of emotional empathy, we're literally in someone else's energetic space. We have left our own aura and are hanging out in our friend's aura. We have intermingled our energies in an effort to be a good friend.

Now that you understand energy and auras, let's take a fresh look at what happens when you jump into someone else's space. Obviously, you're hoping to help that person cope with a painful situation, but the truth is that you may not be helping them at all. If you've lost awareness of your own internal state, or if you're so caught up in your friend's emotional state that you cannot discern your own thoughts and feelings from theirs, then you may actually be doing more harm than good.

Jumping into a friend's aura dilutes your own essence. You're partly in your space, partly in theirs. You're less potent because by intermingling, you've lost part of your own energy. And your friend is probably having a rough time differentiating their own feelings and their own truth from all that foreign energy—your energy—in their space.

I believe that by allowing friends to keep their own energy pristine and clear—even when they're in a painful situation—they'll be able to find the answer that satisfies their own needs, not yours. You would be a much better friend if you empathized from a distance. By consciously staying in your own space—not walking in others' shoes, not feeling their pain—you're able to see other people as they truly are, and from this space of clarity you can offer them your pure empathy and understanding.

As an example, let's say you are out to lunch with a group of friends. The talk turns to one person who will be undergoing minor surgery in the coming days. Most of the people at the table will immediately feel empathy for their friend. The dialogue may be one of commiseration; helpful hints will be offered as to how to this type of operation helped other people recover. All of these comments are meant to be supportive, but the energy attached to the suggestions may be tinged with pity, fear, or a sense of helplessness. Some people will even energetically jump into their friend's space with the intense desire to be of service.

Instead, try staying in your own space and tuning in to your own inner guidance system. Check in with your body and your emotions and ask for the energy of compassion to fill your aura. As this happens, you may be able to pick up on the exact phrase or words that would offer your friend true comfort and peace. Then offer those words to your friend, knowing that you've done your best to avoid sending unwanted judgments and value statements into your friend's auric field.

## Consciously Connecting with Friends

I teach clients to use a tool that helps them keep other people's energies out of their space while still acknowledging that life is all about relating. This tool is called a *protection bubble*, and it encases your aura in a protective layer or wrapper of impenetrable material. The purpose of this covering is to deflect foreign energy coming your way—before it can enter your aura—thus preventing people from unintentionally climbing into your space.

Subconsciously, as two people are relating to each other, they intuitively feel each other's energy and reach into each other's space. As your friend's energy bumps up against your aura, you do not want her to be startled or annoyed that you are no longer allowing her energy into your space, but you do want to give her a gentle psychic reminder that you do not want to co-mingle energies. Let's try it.

---

**EXERCISE 6.1: CREATING YOUR PROTECTION BUBBLE**

1. Sit in meditation with your eyes closed and your feet flat on the floor. Feel your grounding cord and your surrounding aura bubble filled with the energies of peace and stillness.

2. In front of your closed eyes, see an image of yourself sitting in the middle of your aura. Check out the colors of your aura today.

3. Now let's design the protective coating for your aura. You can change the coating every day during your daily meditation, so don't worry that it has to be perfect. Experiment; that's the joy! See what works for you.

4. Think about how you would like to prevent foreign energy from entering your aura. Sometimes I see a fine wire mesh surrounding my aura. This permeable membrane allows my own scattered energies to come in but keeps out others. Other times I envision a platinum coating sealing my aura from all outside influences. You might experiment by surrounding your aura in a bubble of glass or a protective coating of Teflon. You get to choose. Have fun, and fashion a protection bubble of your choosing.

5. When someone thinks of you, the person's energy is coming your way, even from a long distance. Notice what happens to your aura's protection bubble as it encounters outside energy. It may change color as it absorbs this energy, or the energy might just slide off the surface. Notice what you notice.

6. No matter what your protective bubble looks like right now, intend for it to explode in front of you. See it utterly disappear. See your aura in front of you without protection.

7. Create a new protection bubble in front of you. Design it to be just right for you today. Set the intention that it will work for you all day, deflecting any foreign energy before it can enter your aura. When you have it set in place, open your eyes and come out of meditation.

Every day as part of your morning meditation, put a new protection bubble around your aura. Know that it will work for you all day long by turning away foreign energy before it enters your space.

## Attitude, Attitude, Attitude

Although it is a great idea to keep the aura pristine—free from any foreign energy floating around—we are still involved with people every day of our lives. Some of life's greatest lessons are presented to us through the prism of relationships.

We are in relationship with other people, with ourselves, with our job, and with the world at large. Everything is interconnected, and the thoughts, feelings, and emotions that we send out into the world magnetize back to us people, events, and circumstances that are in alignment with how we are in the present moment. The result is not always lollipops and roses. Even that would get old after a while. Relationships are the juice, the fodder, for discovering our innate me-ness. So let's look at the relationships in our world. As we study them, you will come to a greater awareness of the interplay between relationships and life purpose.

Yes, other people are in your life, but only you can choose how to react to them. You can choose your attitude. You can choose each moment of every day.

A shortened version of the following prose about attitude written by Charles Swindoll has hung on my office wall for a number of years. I thought you might like to see the full version from his 1981 radio message series entitled *Strengthening Your Grip*.

## "Attitudes"

The longer I live, the more I realize the importance of choosing the right attitude in life.

Attitude is more important than facts.

It is more important than your past; more important than your education or your financial situation; more important than your circumstances, your successes, or your failures; more important than what other people think or say or do. It is more important than your appearance, your giftedness, or your skills. It will make or break a company. It will cause a church to soar or sink. It will make the difference between a happy home or a miserable home. You have a choice each day regarding the attitude you will embrace.

Life is like a violin. You can focus on the broken strings that dangle, or you can play your life's melody on the one that remains. You cannot change the years that have passed, nor can you change the daily tick of the clock. You cannot change the pace of your march toward your death. You cannot change the decisions or reactions of other people. And you certainly cannot change the inevitable.

Those are strings that dangle!

What you can do is play on the one string that remains—your attitude.

I am convinced that life is 10 percent what happens to me and 90 percent how I react to it.

The same is true for you.

You cannot change events that are happening to you, nor can you change the other person. The only thing you can do is change how you react. You, and no one else, are in charge of your thoughts and emotions. Think back to the branches on your tree of life. See if there is a correlation between the attitude you bring to a specific branch and the strength of that branch.

I would like to suggest that there is only one thing you can change in a relationship, and that is your attitude. You can decide how you react when your boss hands you a task that needs to be completed immediately. Only you can decide if you become aggravated or angry, whether you cuss and scream or whether you remain calm and unruffled. Only you can decide how you want that relationship to develop. You cannot change your boss. However, you are in charge of you. Choosing your thoughts allows you to choose your attitude, and by choosing your attitude, you choose—every moment of every day—the type of relationship you want to experience.

## But How Do I Change My Attitude?

In his book *Man's Search for Meaning,* author Viktor Frankl writes: "Between stimulus and response there is a space. In that space is our power to choose our response. In our response lies our growth and our freedom."

Imprisoned for three years in Auschwitz and other Nazi concentration camps during World War II, Frankl found that he had a choice. He could succumb to the energy surrounding him, or he could choose his own thoughts and feelings. I don't think he knew about grounding cords, auras, or thought forms, yet he saw that his power came from the way he responded to his surroundings. He did not allow his imprisonment to imprison him, he sought freedom and peace within.

Frankl's thoughts and feelings determined his reality. It's not that the concentration camp didn't exist; of course it did. However, he did not succumb to the horror of his surroundings. He found a way to allow his surroundings to exist without being dragged into their bowels. He lived. He wrote. He inspired. He understood that our power lies in that space and time between stimulus and response.

You get to choose. Your life is what you make of it. There is a gap, maybe a nanosecond or two, but still a gap, between the feelings of anger, resentment, or frustration and your reaction to that feeling. See if you can sense that gap. Therein lies your power.

A social media friend was on a rant a while ago about the company she worked for and the horrible things that happened every day. Ten people commented on her rant, agreeing that the company stunk and offering their sympathy. Yes, I get it. The company would never make it onto the "Fifty Best Companies to Work For" list. I also empathized with the anger, the frustration, the screaming-at-the-top-of-her-lungs rage she was expressing. I so wanted to offer fixes to my friend in her moment of need, but I genuinely had only one thing to offer, and I knew it was not what she wanted to hear. I wanted to say, "Go within. Find that space between stimulus and response. That's where attitude lies." Acknowledging that the problem is not out there, but is inside where the work needs to be done, brings a shift in perspective. So I say to you, go within.

---

### EXERCISE 6.2: FINDING THE SPACE
### BETWEEN STIMULUS AND RESPONSE

1. Next time you are ready to explode with an emotion, sit in solitude and go within. Find a quiet, meditative spot and take some deep breaths.

2. Write about your situation and the emotions you are feeling. Write (or type) until your fingers are cramped and your heart is empty. Write it all out, in graphic detail. Get every bit of anger, frustration, and disappointment out of your system.

3. When you feel complete, don't reread what you wrote. That will only return the strong emotion to your body.

4. Feel into your body. Sense your body's quietness, its peace, its calmness.

5. Now hit the delete button and watch as all of those words vanish from your computer screen. If you've

written this out by hand, then tear the paper into little bits and throw them away.

6. Sit in solitude for a moment longer. Let your body become quiet. Take a few deep breaths. Imagine a column of golden light entering the top of your head and filling you with peace, tranquility, and ease.

Remember that we can only change ourselves. In the previous example, the company administrators will continue to do what they do. Treatment of employees may be unfair and perhaps the work environment should be different. Nevertheless, it is not different, and it will not get better just because employees rant and rave. The only thing they truly control is their attitude.

Maybe my friend felt that she was not being heard or valued. Okay, so be it. The company may not value her, but the real question is whether she values herself. She may decide it's time to look for another job, or she may choose to stay and figure out a way to work within the system to bring about some much-needed change. It's up to her. It's up to you. You, and only you, hold the key to your attitude. Remember, life is 10 percent what happens to you and 90 percent how you react to it.

## Preparing for Tough Conversations

Maybe my friend will decide to have a conversation with her boss about the work environment. Maybe you may need to have a talk with one of your coworkers or explain to your teenager why he's grounded. Difficult conversations are just a part of life. Whatever the situation, you can arm yourself with a few energy tools that will make the conversation easier to manage.

Remember the example of entering a room and feeling that the energy was so thick you could cut it with a knife? What if it were the exact opposite? Imagine entering a room full of calm, peaceful, empathetic, crystal-clear energy. Envision how the ensuing difficult conversation might unfold in this environment. You can preset the energy of the room or the dialogue before it happens, and the following exercise shows you how to do it.

---

### EXERCISE 6.3: SETTING THE SPACE

1. Close your eyes, take a deep breath, and imagine yourself in the center of your head—between your ears, behind your eyes. Be in the present moment, clearing any thoughts and emotions from your space.

2. Think of that moment in the future when you will have the difficult discussion. Imagine a bubble floating in front of you that represents that moment. See the colors form in the bubble. These colors represent the energy that you and other people have unconsciously set for this time. Maybe there is some dread or frustration energy in the bubble. Whatever you see, this is the energy currently resonating with this future meeting. However, it does not have to go that way. You can change the vibration of that future event right now. You can set the energy of a future event well in advance, knowing that when the moment comes, the energy will flow.

3. Look again at the bubble in front of you representing this future difficult conversation. Give the bubble a grounding cord. Imagine the dread and frustration leaving that bubble. Watch them drain through the grounding cord.

4. Now add some colors and thoughts to the bubble that represent the qualities you prefer. Maybe you add a color or thought of clarity, calm, and understanding. Set the intention that this moment in time will have affinity with everyone present and that all parties to the conversation will come away with clarity, or truth, or whatever qualities will benefit everyone's growth. See this bubble full of light, clear colors.

5. Now remove the grounding cord and allow this bubble to drift off into the cosmos, knowing that you have set the energy for this future event.

6. Right before you enter that room, imagine your grounding cord around your hips, and set it on maximum release. Cover your aura in its protective coating, knowing that this will help you stay within your own space and prevent others from entering yours. Open your throat chakra. Intend to communicate all that you want to say, clearly and completely. Remember that you have a choice. In that gap between stimulus and response, you can choose your attitude, thereby affecting the outcome of the event. Know that as people enter this meeting space, they will encounter the energy vibrations you have set in place. After the conversation is complete, be sure to fill in with a golden sun of validation and clarity.

There is no time and space when dealing with energies. That is why you can set the energy of the event before it happens. And, while you cannot control how other people in your meeting will be, you can control how you react to the energy they send out.

In the next chapter, we'll continue to work with relationships, but we'll move on to understanding the relationships we have with the most important people in our lives: our family and close friends.

## Energy Pointers

- What color is the energy of your place of employment? Sit in meditation and look at a bubble called "work." See what shows up. Read it.

- What color is the energy of your home? Read it and change what's not working for you.

## Helpful Hints

- Grounding your car is a great way to help you stay focused as you drive around town. You can ground any inanimate object, even your teenager's bedroom! Just refrain from grounding other people, as that is an invasion of their space.

- Setting the space of an upcoming meeting or conversation is a great way to keep the energy on track and focused.

**Chapter 7**

# Shine Bright: Understanding Your Mirrors

We are all meant to shine and to share our natural state of grace with others. Somewhere along the line we have fallen victim to the notion that we can't—we can't be big, we can't stand tall, we can't have our heart's desires. We have dimmed our own light in an effort to accommodate our loved ones, society in general, or those ever-illusive shoulds of life.

It's time to be something different. It's time to let our own light shine. It's time to stand up to our biggest challenges and acknowledge our fears and our uncertainties about who we truly are. It's time to deal with *it* and move on.

### Your Own Reflection: Your Self-Image

I believe that every person carries an image of themselves, a personal magnetic template, in the fourth chakra, the heart center. This template is a miniature version of the way we see ourselves and the beliefs we hold about our world. If we see ourselves as not worthy of love, the template registers "not worthy" and magnetizes to us people, experiences, and events that corroborate our belief. Like attract like. If we believe that people are kind, the template registers that belief and brings kinder people and events into our lives. If you say, "Ugh, it's a horrible day and I hate my job," then it registers unhappiness, anger, or whatever emotion is attached to those thoughts.

Don't despair. You can change the template, the picture of yourself, and thereby change your magnetic pull. So how do you change your template? Well, you have been working on it already. Look in the mirror. Go ahead. Stand in front of a full-length mirror right now. Stop reading and go look in the mirror.

Check on your internal dialogue as you look at yourself. You might find that negative phrases such as "Yuck, I don't like my tummy" or "Wow, I hate my nose" have withered away. Stand tall and say your statement of being with pride and full acknowledgment of who you really are.

If you are still a little hesitant about fully appreciating your body, your mind, your essence, that's okay. Even if there are some negative thoughts still floating around, I imagine they are quite a bit quieter than they were when we started together. No matter how you were raised, what your parents said to you, or what beliefs you hold about your body or your personality, all of those pictures can be erased, if you so choose.

Those pictures are your beliefs. What you believe about yourself becomes what you think about yourself. Thoughts are followed by feelings, and feelings are followed up with action. Therefore, you act in accordance with your beliefs. Your personal magnetic template registers your thoughts, feelings, and beliefs and pulls like-minded energies into your space. This cycle repeats until you challenge a belief through inquiry.

Most often, beliefs form in our subconscious mind. We have been "programmed" by our family, television, advertising, and friends. A story is implanted in a person's psyche about how life should be and what is supposed to happen, and we buy into that story. We believe. For example, our society is obsessed with how women look. Skinny, young, curvy, sexy—all of these thought forms have banded together and are very powerful. The Western world vibrates at a frequency of young and beautiful. If we are not conscious, we can fall into accepting those vibrations, that story, as our own. We soon "believe" that to be beautiful, we must be thin and sexy. Because this is our subconscious belief, we act accordingly. We buy products, we diet, and we wear certain clothes—all because of our belief that thin is beautiful. Really?

By becoming conscious to this underlying belief, we can question it. We can hold that belief up to our statement of being and decide if we really believe that thin is the only beautiful. That is questioning a belief. Consciously.

As we unravel this belief, we change the vibration, the frequency, of our thoughts. We are no longer drawing to us, without question, thoughts of "I must be thin. I'm too fat. Life is horrible because I'm not a size two." If we consciously change our belief, we attract new thoughts, new vibrations, to our space. Our template becomes different. We become different. We act differently, we verbalize different statements; we *are* different.

As an example, one of my beliefs is that I should go to the gym regularly. But I haven't. As I think about my belief, I realize a couple of things. First, this is really a "should." I tell myself, "I should go to the gym today." I'm not excited about it. The emotion in my body is heavy and draggy when I think "I should go to the gym regularly." That dragging-energy feeling is what keeps me from exercising.

Next, I question my belief that "I have to go to the gym." I realize I don't have to go to the sports club to exercise, but the underlying belief that it's important to exercise is valid and fair.

It's the should that gets me down. I exercise by shoveling snow in the winter and hiking in the summer. That counts. Maybe I don't need to go to the gym at all. I am able to re-phrase my belief as "Exercise is good for my health." There's not a should to be found in that statement. Yes, exercise is good for my health, but I am not in judgment when I do not exercise regularly. I have changed my core belief. I have dropped the should and all the draggy energy associated with the thought that "I should go to the gym." My new belief is in alignment with my Spirit. I feel the energy in my body shift to a lighter, higher vibration. I bring more enthusiasm to the statement "Exercise is good for my health." Consequently, I am more likely to include some form of exercise in my daily routine.

As you remove this old programming of who you think you should be and what you think you should do, you are coming into alignment with your statement of being. Your new beliefs will send ripples of newness throughout your aura. Your thoughts will be different, your feelings will be different, and the actions you take in the world will also be new and different. You will come closer and closer to being a vibrational match with your Highest and Best Self.

Let's do an exercise to cement that new personal magnetic template of yourself into your fourth chakra, your heart center.

---

### EXERCISE 7.1: YOUR TEMPLATE:
### YOUR FOURTH CHAKRA

1. Sit in a comfortable chair, with your feet flat on the floor and your eyes closed. Sit and breathe in peace and stillness. Be in the space in the center of your head, grounded and at ease. Breathe in and out, sinking deeper into your chair with each exhale.

2. Now imagine standing in front of an exact duplicate of you. Picture your twin self coming into focus. See a clear, clean, crisp image of your full body, exactly as you look today. See your legs, your arms, your torso, and your smile. If you find it hard to visualize all your features, then step out of meditation to go look at yourself in a full-length mirror.

3. This duplicate has the same hairstyle, the same eyes, the same nose, and the same fingernails. Look down and see if this image is wearing the same color of socks that you have on today.

4. If you need to step out of meditation again, do so. Go look at yourself again in the mirror. Really look. Stare,

in fact. Say hello and send some loving thoughts to your mirror image. Now go back to your meditative state.

5. Look again at that template of yourself. Make sure the image really, truly looks like you. Look deep into your soul eyes. See kindness, see joy. What quirky personality traits make you be you? Validate those unique qualities that differentiate you from your next-door neighbor.

6. Think of how much baggage you've let go of since we started this journey together. Have this image reflect your updated version of who you truly are, right now, today.

7. Once you feel that your personal magnetic template is an exact duplicate of who you are right now, imagine reaching out and pulling that image closer to your physical body. Pull it into your heart, your fourth chakra. Place it right in the middle of your heart space. Feel the image anchor, solid and secure.

8. Come out of meditation and read your statement of being aloud. Feel that statement come alive in your body. Own it. Be it. Integrate it. This newly updated personal magnetic template is your beacon, calling to you all energies that are in alignment with your vibration.

As you go about the activities of your day, be conscious of your thoughts and words. Spend time reflecting on whether they represent the new you or the old you. Become comfortable with this new image of yourself. Know that as you integrate this image into your life, your thoughts will change, your beliefs about yourself will change, and then your actions will change. You are on the way to living a life full of events and circumstances that are in alignment with the shining light that you are.

When you come across a belief that no longer serves you, get rid of it. Tap it out, send it down your grounding cord, or blow it up in a rose. You have tools now. Use them.

## Mirror, Mirror: Family Reflections

The people in our lives are our mirrors. Through the prism of their actions and our reactions, we view ourselves. Think about the significant people in your life. They are your teachers and your mentors. You are attracted to the people who have qualities you want to experience. Your spouse is kind because you have kindness in you. Your brother-in-law pushes your buttons when he is bossy because you attracted the lesson of learning to express your own feelings and not be trampled by someone else's views. Each person in your life is here for a reason. Your daughter's rebelliousness is an opportunity to test your own need to be in control. She is your mirror. The lesson is within you. The opportunity to grow is yours. Will you take it?

Generally your Spirit chooses a childhood that promotes the development of the challenges you are ready to face. As an example, if you have chosen the theme of learning to open up to love, then you may have parents who don't display their love in an open manner. They may be reserved and closed-hearted. If you want to learn more about being safe in the world, you may have experienced moments of being unsafe. Most of us learn our major lessons by first experiencing the opposite side of the equation, or who we are not. The absence of love, say during childhood, may be the necessary precursor to acknowledging later on in life the importance of love. The absence of safety allows us an opportunity to acknowledge times when we do feel safe. Other common themes revolve around learning to speak our own truth, not looking to others for approval, and developing compassion.

This next exercise offers clues to the people—the mirrors—helping you to understand some of your major challenges.

---

### EXERCISE 7.2: YOUR MOST IMPORTANT MIRRORS

1. In your journal, list the top five people who have had an impact on your life. Often we think of our parents, our siblings, and our life partners. You may find, however, that you also include others such as a mentor or your best friend.

2. Next to each person on the list, write their top five positive and negative traits. Be as fair and unbiased as possible. For example, if one of your father's positive traits is honesty, then that trait may have influenced your life and landed on your list of heart traits. On the other hand, your father's impatience may have made you feel insecure and unheard. Maybe your mother's positive trait of not caring what other people think helps you to understand how you react in various circumstances. You will have ten traits for each person, five positive and five negative. This is not as easy as it sounds, so take your time.

3. Look for common threads among the five people, and think about how those threads have impacted your life and the decisions you have made.

4. Now spend some time getting to the root of the "whys." Consider why these particular people are such strong influences and facilitators to your growth. For example, let's say that a couple of your primary people possess the trait of being judgmental. As you examine the impact of this on your own life, you realize that the judgments they hold have caused you to spend an inordinate amount of energy trying to gain their approval. Your challenge may be to learn to look within for validation and not be overly concerned with the thoughts and feelings of others. On the other hand, suppose you find that your older brother and your mother offer significant clues to some of your most intense inner-critic statements. Maybe your brother's bullying led you to feel insecure and unsafe in the world. You also realize that while you admire your mother's meek and mild manner, you also see that she was unable to express her needs fully and completely. You realize that, put together, these two mirrors offer you a glimpse into why you are afraid to speak your mind. It could be that your challenge is to open up your fifth chakra (your voice/throat) and speak your truth, even in the face of opposition from others.

5. In your journal, write about your observations.

The people in your life allow you to experience certain emotional triggers in order to advance your learning around one of your life's challenges. They are your mirrors, reflecting back to you aspects of yourself that you want to enhance or heal. Maybe you have already started down the road of healing. Your personal magnetic template is now in place, registering who you really are, right now, in present time. Think about whether some of the lessons you've learned from the people in your life are now complete. Could it be that you still view some of your mirrors through the lens of the old you? Consider whether it would be wise to update your thoughts and feelings about some of the people in your life. You also have played a major role in the lives of each of these people. Spend some time thinking about how you have helped each of them to understand their major life challenges.

Let's say that you realize your sister is one of your mirrors, but you are still a little unsure of the exact nature of the lesson to be learned through your relationship with her. After some reflection, you realize that your sister pushes your invalidation button. You do not feel heard. You feel her judgment and criticism, and you react by being rebellious and stubborn. You know that your reaction is out of proportion to the situation. You are triggered emotionally, and you lash out in a way that feels right in the moment, but deep down in your gut, you know that you are acting like a five-year-old.

Own it. Own the childishness. Own your own reaction. This is not about what your sister said or did to push your button. The next time this happens, remember that space between stimulus and response. Pause and consider how you would like to react. Consider how she is mirroring back to you a quality that is challenging to you.

Choose to stay out of drama, to stay out of the story of why *she* caused *you* to react this way. Decide what attitude you will bring to this situation. Deal with this from a place of compassion as you work to uncover the clues to one of your major lessons.

If you find yourself standing toe to toe with your sister in the midst of a heated exchange, pause and use some of your tools to diffuse the situation and get yourself back into alignment with who you really are. You could check your grounding cord. Then make sure your aura is filled with your own energy and is surrounded with a protection bubble, preventing your sister's energy from invading your space. You could blow up a rose, sending invalidation, anger, and stubbornness out of your aura. You could watch those energies leave your system. You might see the colors of anger at not being heard fill up the rose. And finally, you could ask the golden sun to gather all the scattered parts of you—maybe you left some in your sister's space—and return that energy to you. As you pop that sun and replenish your body and aura with your own essence, be sure to give yourself lots of encouragement and validation for actually using your tools in the middle of a heated discussion. High-five yourself. Bring some amusement into your aura. Feel nurtured and at peace.

Later on, you could do a tapping exercise, telling the story of this argument until you feel a bodily shift, releasing the last remnants of any emotional charge. Whatever tool you use, spend time being kind to yourself, because this is a lesson, and your sister is one of your strongest mirrors. Be amused and learn what this interaction had to teach you.

This is not easy. The graduate-level curriculum in energy awareness surely resides in the relationships we have with our family members, specifically our parents and siblings. When dealing with family-of-origin dynamics, it's so easy to lose our space, to become ungrounded, to forget to put on our protection bubble. Our family members are in our lives to push our buttons, to call us out on our behavior, allowing us to experience deeper levels of growth and knowingness.

The wounds may be deep on both sides of the relationship, but it *is* possible to make headway, at least on your own end. Remember that the significant people in your life are acting as your mirrors, reflecting back to you some of the not-so-pleasant parts of your personality so that you may come to know yourself on a deeper, wiser level. Do not be in judgment of these parts of you. We all have areas we're not proud of, but you now have tools to remove some of other people's judgments and criticisms from your space.

Once you understand that what you put out you get back, you'll become aware of your reactions as you relate to your mirrors. The objective is to deal with these relationships from a space of openness, not hostility and fearfulness.

Let's say that you and your father have a tumultuous relationship. You may not be speaking to each other, and there is an undercurrent of drama during holiday dinners. You each feel hurt and invalidated. You both want to blame the other for the lack of affinity between you. Your father is your mirror, and you are his. Remember that you can't change your father; you can only change your own attitude about how you relate to your father. You set the tone of how you think and feel. You may not be able to affect the way your father feels about you *just yet*, but let's say that you are ready to change how you feel about him.

Use your tools. Remember that you have a choice in how you react. In that nanosecond between stimulus and response, you get to choose. You could elect to relate from the space of the five-year-old who is hurt, broken, and judged to be not good enough. Or you could decide to react from the space of *now*—the person you are in the present moment.

Energy flows between family members, even if they are separated by a great distance. You can be miles apart, but the energy—the vibration—you send out will be felt by the other person. Whether they choose to accept your new-found state of beingness is up to them. You cannot change the other person. You cannot force them into harmony with your own perspective. However, you can stand in your own truth—with your thoughts and feelings vibrating in love, compassion, openness, and peace. Your family member may feel that vibration and choose to accept it, or they might still be in the middle of drama, needing to be right, needing to be validated, and unconsciously choose not to match your vibration. Either way, send some gentle kindness their way. You do not need to talk with them; just send them compassion and allow them to be the way they are.

If you find that you need an extra-heavy-duty protection bubble to catch all the energy whacks your family sends your way, then live in a heavily protected aura for a while. Be in command of your own space and the energy that flows through your aura and your body. You do not have to be in resistance to the energy of your family; in fact, it's best if you just let judgments and criticisms pass without comment. What you resist persists, so simply allow your loved ones to be who they are. Concentrate on yourself, on your reaction, on the thoughts and feelings that you're sending out into the world. Concentrate on understanding the "whys" of some of your major life lessons.

Remember, you get to choose. Every moment of every day.

## The Looking Glass of Experiences

How we react to certain emotional circumstances may also act as a mirror, reflecting back to us opportunities to experience some major life lessons. Most of us have had the experience of having an emotional reaction that is out of proportion to the triggering event. The next time this happens, pause and think of why you responded this way and consider the underlying message. Are you not being heard? If so, what does that tell you about your need for outside approval and validation?

---

### EXERCISE 7.3: UNDERSTANDING AN
### OVER-THE-TOP EMOTION

1. Sit in meditation. Be grounded to the earth and locate yourself in the center of your head. Feel yourself come to that place of stillness as you breathe in and out.

2. Bring some earth energy up through your feet. Feel it swirl around in your first chakra before cascading out the back. Now bring in some cosmic energies from above your head. Visualize those energies falling down the back of your body, entering your first chakra and mixing with the earth energy. Now feel this mixture move up the front of your body until it spouts out the top of your head like a whale. Notice that some of the earth/cosmic mixture branched off at your throat and is moving down your arms, your wrists, and to your palms, where it spouts forth.

3. Feel gratitude for your newfound ability to bring your body and aura to stillness. Acknowledge how far you've come in understanding how the thoughts and feelings of others affect your energetic system. Be in awe of your ability to see and read the colors of energies. You are doing it! Be proud of your progress.

4. Sit in this place of stillness, breathe, and just be.

5. Bring into your awareness instances when your emotions were out of proportion to the situation. For example, perhaps you were on the phone with a customer service representative of a large corporation, and you became angry and yelled at the man on the other end of the line. You were not specifically angry at him, yet you found yourself expressing anger in a way that was totally out of proportion to the circumstances.

6. As you recall this experience, ask yourself why you reacted in such an over-the-top manner. Maybe you

expressed anger because you were not being understood or validated. Perhaps you felt that the large company really didn't care about you, and your reaction to powerlessness was an emotional outburst.

7. Now think of another situation when your reaction to an incident was out of proportion. This time, instead of recalling a situation that involved anger, perhaps you remember feeling a deep, searing pain in your stomach (your third chakra, your power center) the day you got stuck in traffic and were late to pick up your child from school. This type of situation, while frustrating, usually does not cause you to emotionally break down, but this time it did. You cried, you yelled, you honked the horn in frustration, all the time acknowledging that this was a very atypical response. Ask yourself why you reacted this way. Maybe you remember that on that day you had been caught unprepared during a client meeting. You were embarrassed, and your inner critic was berating you as you drove to your son's school. You realize that you felt powerless in the client meeting and also in the traffic jam. Both incidents triggered an emotional response of not being in control. Maybe this is one of your major challenges during this lifetime: to stand in your own power, regardless of the circumstances.

8. Come out of meditation and think about what emotional triggers you face. Journal your thoughts. Come up with an overarching theme, some major life challenge that you are experiencing.

Some people have very difficult challenges to overcome, such as physical abuse, chronic pain, or serious illness. Others have less obvious challenges, such as overcoming a fear of abandonment or allowing themselves to open up to love.

Maybe you realize that you are not what your family thinks you should be. They may be full of judgments and value statements about who they *think* you are, but your lesson is to stand tall, speak your own truth, and not allow the poisoned arrows of expectation to define who you are. On the other hand, maybe someone you love has hurt you deeply, and as a result, you have closed off your heart to others. It might be time to open up, be vulnerable again, and stand in love.

Review your thoughts and determine if there is an overarching theme. Some examples might be:

- If you believe that you are the black sheep of the family—the untouchable, the outcast—then your overarching theme might be to realize that you are worthy, that you do belong. By looking to other people as your only source of validation, you have missed the beauty of your own bright light.

- If your overarching theme is to open your heart and express your vulnerability, then your mirror may have been the person or situation that closed your heart in the first place.

- If your overarching theme is to learn to speak your truth and stand in your power, then the person who pushes your button may be the one who controls your time or your money.

Remember to validate yourself as you review your work. We all have mirrors; we all have challenges. This is about coming to terms with the "whys." In addition, once we understand the mirrors in our life, we are inches away from uncovering our life purpose.

Our challenge is to be our authentic self. Always. Taming our inner critic allows us to stand in our own truth instead of listening to the judgments, criticisms, and thoughts of others that keep us small. Our task is to rise above the pettiness of who said what to whom and how they made us feel. Our task is to shine bright amidst the arrows of energetic whacks and jealous outbursts of others. As we do so, we offer others a model of how it might be. Just think what the world would be like if we all manifested the splendor of shining bright as we stand in our own brilliance!

---

### EXERCISE 7.4: MEDITATION:
### LOOKING THROUGH THE MIRROR OF LOVE

1. Sit in silence for a moment. Be in the center of your head. Be grounded, with your feet flat on the floor and your protection bubble surrounding your aura. Ask for some earth energy to come up through your legs, enter your first chakra, and waterfall out the back, returning to the earth in a cycle. Feel your feet planted solidly on the floor. Intend for some cosmic energy to enter the seventh chakra. Feel the energy slide down your back and mix with the earth energy in your first chakra. Imagine this mixture coming up the front of your body, spouting out the top of your head, and swirling around your aura. Intend for these

neutral energies to connect you to the earth and the cosmos.

2. Sit in this space of peace for a moment.

3. Imagine a world in which you are brilliant, gorgeous, talented, and fabulous. See it. Feel it.

4. Visualize a soap bubble in front of you, and imagine that bubble filling with all your brilliance. Imagine what your world would look like if you were BIG. See it. Feel it. Be it. Add some colors to your bubble, colors that represent being fabulous, being brilliant, being full of love for yourself and others.

5. Make your bubble bigger. Give all those fantastic colors and feelings room to move around. See them flowing, moving, oscillating back and forth.

6. Ground your bubble and allow all foreign energies, all thoughts of limitation and staying small, to leave the bubble. Know that those thoughts are not yours; they are the expectations of others in your life. Allow all that energy to run down the bubble's grounding cord.

7. Feel yourself full of peace and knowingness. We are all meant to shine bright, to be brilliant reminders of Spirit. Bring some golden light, representing your Highest and Best Self, into that bubble.

8. When you have your bubble big, brilliant, and full of the right colors and feelings, remove the grounding cord and bring the bubble into your heart center. Update your personal magnetic template with this image of your Highest and Best Self. Know that you

are a beautiful, brilliant light. Shine bright. Be brilliant. Be BIG.

9. When you are ready, come out of meditation knowing that your heart chakra is pulsing with the vibration of you, powerful beyond measure.

## Energy Pointers

- In your daily meditation, choose a different color for your earth energy. Experiment with lime green to see what that feels like. Then move to powder blue. Try out a mixture of pale pink and pale yellow. Choose your favorite.

## Helpful Hints

- What you think and feel you will be. See yourself as your best friend or lover sees you. Smile!

- As you wake up each morning, say the following phrase (or your own version) to yourself: "Good morning, sweet pea! You are mighty fine!" Smile and know that you are great.

# Part II:

# Living Your Life on Purpose

## Chapter 8

# Living on Purpose Key #1: Havingness

Up until now, you have worked on your relationship with yourself and other people. You have learned that it really is all about you. You have the power to choose your own reality by attending to your thoughts and emotions. Living a life free of other people's energies becomes a daily practice of grounding, staying in your own space, setting your attitude, understanding your mirrors, and consciously choosing your thoughts and feelings.

As we tune in to our own internal truths, we become less concerned with the shoulds of the world. What our neighbor or a family member thinks takes a back seat to our own internal wisdom. We have a purpose, a unique gift that we are destined to share with the world. It's time to move our focus toward uncovering this purpose and creating a life that is in alignment with our internal essence, our Spirit.

I believe there are four keys to living our lives on purpose, and I will devote a chapter to each. The first key is *havingness*: our ability to "have" this new life. When we are in a state of havingness, we are satisfied, content, creative, and living a life in alignment with our statement of being. We are comfortable with our current state of affairs, yet at the same time we acknowledge that we can have more. This is the dichotomy of havingness: accepting what is and wanting more.

We've all heard stories of people who won the lottery, yet within a few years their money was gone and they returned to their pre-lottery lifestyle. Likewise, there are people who rose too fast in the corporate world, and just when life was wonderful, they crashed and burned. These are examples of people unable to "have" their newfound status. They probably believed they didn't deserve to live the life of their dreams. Maybe their inner-critic voice was constantly reminding them of times they had tried and failed in business or spent a week's pay on a frivolous shopping spree. They needed tools. They needed what you have—a way of consciously keeping your internal dialogue from sabotaging your newfound ways. Later in this chapter, we'll learn ways to enhance our capability of havingness, and we'll do an exercise that will take us up the ladder from a low to a high state of havingness. But first, let's remove the impediments to accepting life as it is, right here in this moment.

## What You Resist Persists

Most people spend an inordinate amount of time making action plans, striving toward the next mark, pushing, reaching, and then going on vacation to get away from all of the stress and pressure. They cannot "have" their current state of affairs. They are in resistance to it, and what we resist persists. Dreams are important, but so is being very conscious and present in the life that we have right now.

Being in havingness is accepting, with gratitude, the fullness of your life, just as it is, right here, right now, including the not-so-good parts. If you resist who you are right now, you are in a state of lack, not abundance. You have sent the signal "I am resisting this. Send me more of the same." As an example, let's say that you are single and not happy about the situation. You find yourself constantly wishing, hoping, and dreaming of finding a life partner. Your days are spent thinking about the future or rehashing the past. If you are energetically "out there" searching for a mate, you cannot be fully present in your everyday life. You cannot have your current state of being single. You are sending the message to the universe "I'm searching for a mate." And guess what? The universe sends you energy of the same vibration: searching.

On the other hand, maybe you live far away from family and friends and are wishing and hoping for the day when you can move back home. As you pine away for what you are missing, think about whether you are energetically "here" or "there." It might be that there are lots of activities and friends to be made in your current city if you decided to have your current situation.

Bring to mind something in your life that you are resisting right now. If you frequently think, "When such and such happens, I will be happy (or free, or out of debt, or not so alone)," you are resisting your present-time reality. Let's work on that. Write down five things that you would like to change about your life. Maybe you don't like your boss, or your apartment, or your roommate.

---

### EXERCISE 8.1: YOUR RESISTANCE
### TO CURRENT CIRCUMSTANCES

The first key to living a life full of purpose and meaning is to be able to have where we are right now. Once we are comfortable with our current circumstances, then we are able to take a step toward more. This exercise highlights those areas of our life where we have "low havingness," an inability to be content with our present-time reality.

1. List the top five things that irk you.

2. Spend some time honestly assessing where you are in resistance to your current circumstances. You may be dreaming of a time when life will be different or constantly regretting something you did in the past. Consider whether you are so busy planning your future that you are missing the joys of today.

3. Once you have completed the list, use your tools to remove the associated thoughts and feelings from your aura. You might want to refer to exercise 2.3 to tap the story of why you are unhappy out of your system. You might want to put the energy of discontent in a rose and blow up the rose. Or you can send that old baggage of why your life is not the way you want it down your grounding cord. Whatever tool works best for you, use it.

Now ask yourself, "Am I happy with things just the way they are, right now, without exception?" Let's say your answer is "yes, I'm happy with the home I live in, and my husband and kids are great, but my sister, with her constantly derogatory comments about my life choices, is driving me crazy." You are in a state of appreciation of most things, but you are in a state of resistance to at least a portion of your life: your sister and the judgments she holds. Remember, she is your mirror, and she is offering you a chance to get to know a part of you that is asking to be experienced.

To move from resistance to appreciation, take a step back and look at the situation from a place of neutrality. As we detach from emotional drama, we can see ourselves honestly and not be tripped up by the stories that we have told ourselves—perhaps for years and years.

In this example, your sister has not changed at all, but you, in your neutral state of detachment, have shifted your perspective. Your attitude is different, and that is the point. You are no longer focused on what you do not want—in this case, reacting to your sister's constant criticism of your life. You have moved from a grumbling state of mind, which has a lower vibration, to the higher-vibrational frequency of allowance and appreciation. You have removed yourself from the drama. Through neutrality, you can stand back and look at the circumstances in a completely new light.

You may not condone your sister's behavior, and you may not even like her, but you can accept her exactly as she is, with neutrality. That is moving from resistance to acceptance. You cannot escape from your life by wishing and hoping for your fairy godmother to magically whisk you away to a better life. That's resistance, too.

Havingness is accepting life exactly as it is, right at this moment. It is being in present time, with all of our emotional baggage. It's also about being grateful for the lessons we're learning from that baggage. Yes, that's right. Be grateful for the messes, the pain, the hurt, or the abandonment you feel. Acknowledge it. Don't run away from it. See it. Make peace with what is. Be in the present moment and appreciate with gratitude all parts of your life.

Spending time in gratitude for all that is going well in life is also important. The more attention we place on the positive aspects of any situation, the more we magnetize to us similar thoughts, feelings, and circumstances. This is not a Pollyanna way of being. There are many scientific studies that show that being grateful for what is going well in our lives actually raises the level of our "happiness quotient."

## Grace

Lao Tzu, a wise poet and philosopher of ancient China, is often quoted as saying, "Be content with what you have; rejoice in the way things are. When you realize there is nothing lacking, the whole world belongs to you." When we realize that nothing is lacking, we experience appreciation, gratitude, prosperity, and abundance. When we feel these emotions deeply—when we wake up with them and go to sleep with them—then our outer world matches our inner world. What we feel, we will be. Our thoughts and feelings of prosperity and abundance magnetize to us all the material things that represent that prosperity and abundance.

Grace is that sweet spot: accepting without resistance our current state of being, with all its ups and downs, disappointments and discouragements; having exactly where we are right now, for the rest of our lives.

Think about that for a long moment. Contemplate accepting without resistance exactly where you are, with all the discomfort you may feel about your financial situation, your job, or your relationships, for the rest of your life. As you stop the striving for that which is outside of you and become content with the current state of your existence, you come into alignment with the vibration of havingness. As you accept, deep within your soul, that you are exactly where you should be at this time doing exactly what is best for you, then in that moment of acceptance is grace.

This is the miracle: grace. Grace removes the feelings of lack. Grace is a state of prosperity and abundance. It is a non-striving, totally aware, totally creative space of havingness. In this state of grace, you are ready to create. You are ready to magnetize to you all the material things that represent this state of appreciation and prosperity, and we will do this by creating a mock-up. We will discuss mock-ups, another key to living a life on purpose, in chapter 10, but for now, meditate on "having" exactly where you are right now.

You might be asking yourself, "How do I really get to the place of living in feelings of appreciation, gratitude, prosperity, and abundance?" The answer: you have already been working on it with the exercises I've outlined. Removing negative self-talk, learning to see yourself through the prism of relationships, being in a state of gratitude, accepting all parts of your life (even the not-so-wonderful parts), understanding that resistance can be moved—all of this is allowing you to be the best version of yourself. Living your life on purpose is being this state of grace.

---

### EXERCISE 8.2: BE, DO, HAVE

1. Make a list of twenty things that you want to be, do, or have. You might want to learn to sing on key or play the piano. You might want to go back to school or have a bigger home. You might want to be less frustrated when talking with your aging parent or to be friendlier to a new neighbor.

2. After you have made your list, sit in meditation. Keep your feet flat on the floor, close your eyes, and be in the center of your head. Check to make sure your grounding cord is in place and your aura is clean and clear.

3. Now think of the first item on your "Be, Do, Have" list. Let's say you want a new home. You are tired of living in your current cramped quarters, and you really, really want to have a larger home. Imagine an energy bubble out in front of your closed eyes. Intend for this bubble to show you the current state of havingness around this desire for a new home. Maybe you've been dreaming of this new home for some time. See the colors in the bubble. Maybe the bubble is full of other people's wants and desires. Check to see if this is your energy or someone else's. Maybe your partner wants to stay in your existing home and there's some struggle energy in that bubble. Or perhaps you realize that the wispy fantasy nature

of your bubble reminds you that this desire to have a new home is more of a dream right now. Whatever you see, don't judge it, just look. This is the state of your havingness around this item.

4. Now ask yourself, "How much can I 'have' my current situation? How much can I 'have' the current home I live in?" See a number pop into your awareness representing the percentage that you can "have" your current situation. Maybe the number is 20 percent. You are 20 percent okay with having your current home.

5. Put a grounding cord on this bubble and drain out the energies that are not yours. Drain out your partner's struggle energy. Drain out your own fantasy energy. Drain out any judgment energy or disappointment energy of where you currently are in your havingness.

6. When your bubble is clear, ask yourself again, "How much can I 'have' my current state of being?" Imagine a number in front of you. Maybe instead of 20 percent, you can "have" your current state of being 50 percent of the time. Very little will change until you are at peace, 100 percent of the time, with your current level of havingness around this desire. Until you let go of the grasping, striving, wishing, or hoping, it's hard to take a step toward the new. Add some acceptance energy to your bubble. Be sure that any striving or craving energies are gone. Add some peace, contentment, and wonderment energy to your bubble. Be in acceptance of where you are right now.

7. When you are at 100 percent acceptance of your current situation, intend for that energy to infuse your aura with your new level of havingness. Come out of meditation.

Havingness is a dichotomy of two very different states: having exactly where you are at the moment while acknowledging that life is all about moving forward—wanting more. You've worked the space of accepting, with gratitude, exactly where you are right now, but that doesn't mean you must stay here for the rest of your life.

Once you know that all is well, right here, right now, you are ready to take a step into something new, something larger, something more. So what do you want?

The next exercise is adapted from two very different sources: Esther and Jerry Hicks' *The Teachings of Abraham* and Boulder Psychic Institute's Avatar class on money and manifesting. I have taken a little from each and combined them into an exercise designed to help you move up the ladder of havingness.

---

### EXERCISE 8.3: REMOVING WANTER'S BLOCK

This exercise will shift your want from your current state of havingness to a higher state of havingness, clearing any blocks along the way. We will use the image of a ladder with twelve rungs. Each rung will represent a statement that moves you closer to your desire and removes any wanter's block from having your new state of havingness.

1. Pick an item from your list of twenty things you want to be, do, or have. Let's stay with the theme of wanting a new home, but let's change it up a little bit. Let's say that you want to spend your winters on the island of Maui in a home of your own. When you think that thought, alarm bells sound throughout your body and aura, as if to say, "That's too big a want. I can't do that." This is not just any move to a bigger home, this is out of your current realm of comfort. You have "wanter's block." Your want is bigger than your current state of havingness.

2. The first step is to identify what you want. In this example, you want to live in Hawaii during the winter. In your journal, draw a circle at the top of the page. In this circle, write the words "I spend my winters in my home on Maui." That is your focus. Write your sentence in the present tense to bring it into your current state of havingness. You will work your way up the ladder of havingness, setting your vibration at higher and higher levels until you reach the top rung on your ladder. At that point you will be able to "have" the statement "I spend my winters in my home on Maui."

3. Now, in your journal, draw a picture of a ladder with twelve rungs, and number each rung, with one at the bottom of the page and twelve at the top. You will come up with twelve statements, each a baby step closer in havingness to the wanted desire, "I spend my winters in my home on Maui."

4. On the bottom rung of your ladder, find one statement that fits within your current level of havingness. Let's say that statement is "Hawaii winter weather is warm and gentle." You feel comfortable with that statement. Write that statement on the bottom rung.

5. Move up one rung and write out another statement that moves you a little bit closer to the statement at the top of your page. This time, the statement "There are many ways to spend winters on Maui" seems about right. It's comfortable; you can "have" that statement, and it's a baby step closer to your goal. Keep moving up the rungs of your havingness ladder. Maybe your next phrase is "Many ordinary people have second homes in Hawaii," and the following phrase is "Lots of people rent out their homes when they are not on the island, bringing in some extra money to defray expenses." Then another statement might be "There are condos for sale on Maui right now that are close to my price range." Yet another is "I know that my limiting thoughts can be cleared away," which is followed by "I am increasing my havingness space just by doing this exercise." The next statement is "It will be exciting to watch the universe bring me my winter home in Hawaii," then another is "I don't have to buy a place; I could just rent one, or maybe do a home exchange." Rung 10 might be "It might be possible to rent out my home on the mainland while I'm in Hawaii," and rung 11 might be "It *is* possible for me to spend my winters in Hawaii." Then finally, rung 12 says, "I can have this. I feel it's possible. I

don't have to know how just yet. This is about removing the blocks to having my Maui home, so bring it on, universe."

6. Finding the first statement is usually easy, but somewhere in the middle of the process, you might find that it's hard to move forward. Pause for a moment and acknowledge whose voice is in your head. Visualize a rose, call all the shoulds of your parents or your neighbors into the rose, and then blow up that rose. Use your tools to calm your inner critic and move forward. Or instead of blowing a rose, you could just pause and quietly acknowledge your inner critic's need to be heard. Whatever tool works for you, use it. Then move on. Continue climbing higher and higher on your havingness ladder. Each time you move up a rung, you are increasing your vibration around having your statement. You'll notice an increased level of excitement and believability as you find new statements. You may even notice a shift in your body as the wanter's block releases.

7. When you've finished, compare how you felt when you started to the way you feel at the end. You don't need to know how you will manifest this winter home in Hawaii, you simply must be able to "have" it.

The dichotomy of havingness is being content with your current life while wanting something better. You are neither grasping nor striving. You are in a state of expectancy. Your hands are cupped, waiting to receive. In this state of quiet anticipation, you are in the vibration of havingness. You are in the state of grace. Remember, you don't manifest what you desire, you manifest who or what you are. The being state is the most important factor in how we manifest the life of our dreams. It really is all about be-ing. The do-ing, the active part, will show up as a result of the way you think and feel.

## Energy Pointers

- What color is the energy of tranquility to you?

- In your daily meditation, choose a different color for your cosmic energy. Experiment with sky blue. Then move to royal blue. Try out a mixture of pale orange and pale yellow. Choose your favorite.

## Helpful Hints

- Remember to keep working with golden suns to replenish yourself. Sit for three minutes and do nothing but fill yourself with the warm, radiant energy of golden suns. Notice how you feel afterward.

- Review Exercise 4.3: Picturing Your Dream Life. Continue finding images that represent the feeling states of joy, tranquility, and delight. You are almost ready to open those manila envelopes, so get busy.

### Chapter 9

# Living on Purpose Key #2: The Energy of Money

As you move deeper into your understanding of how to live a life full of purpose and meaning, it is time to become comfortable with the second key, the energy of money. Yes, money is energy—a form of energy that you receive in exchange for contributions you make in the world. Most people, though, are not conscious of how money energy moves through their lives.

As a society, we have tons of *pictures*, or stories, built up around money. Passed down from our ancestors, these stories are lodged deep within our psyche and form the cornerstone of our current belief system around money. You might say that money is "dirty" or "the root of all evil." You might not even realize that these phrases color your view of this neutral force of energy.

Money is a means of exchange. That is all. By stripping away the feelings and emotions surrounding money and embracing its energy as a tool, you are able to use this powerful source of potentiality to fuel your life of purpose. The first stop in harnessing this tool's power is to become conscious of how you speak about money. Let's go back to an exercise used at the very beginning of this book.

You will use a name web again (see exercise 2.1), this time focusing on how you view money. In the middle circle on the name web, you will write the word "Money" and then quickly write down all the associations you have when you think about money. You might reflect upon:

- some of your mother's favorite phrases about money.
- some of your father's favorite phrases about money.
- how you feel about money.
- whether you think money is dirty.
- whether you have to work hard and struggle to get ahead.
- whether you believe money is the root of all evil.
- whether you believe spiritual people should or shouldn't be wealthy or affluent.
- whether you believe money is rewarded to those who live by certain rules.

---

**EXERCISE 9.1: CREATE A NAME WEB**
**FOR YOUR MONEY LIFE**

1. Draw a circle and create a name web around the topic of money.

2. As you did in exercise 2.1, draw circles around the words or phrases with a repetitive tone or mood. There may be themes of struggle, lack, envy, or striving. Maybe you see words representing dreamy fantasies of what money can do for you.

3. Write those repeating themes off to the side of your web.

This web represents your current level of thought and emotion around the concept of money. It is your personal model of how you see yourself connecting with the energy of money. This web acts as a filter, drawing to you events and circumstances that match the frequency of your story around money. As you review your web, consider:

- what your web reveals about your relationship with money.
- whether this is a current representation of how you see money or one based in childhood memories.

Reflect upon your current relationship with money. Start the process of stripping away other people's thoughts and feelings. Dig deep.

One common way people deal with the energy of money is that they don't deal with it at all. If you've ever come home from the mall with a bag full of shoes or clothes that you don't need, you've become unconscious to your money energy. Another example of this problem is "forgetting" to pay your bills on time.

If you find yourself literally closing your eyes or shutting down your emotions when the topic of money arises, put that unconscious energy into a rose and blow up that rose. Tell the story of how you went on a shopping spree and spent all that money. Get to the core issue. Find out why, and then move the energy. Get it out of your system.

Somewhere, at some time, a belief formed in your subconscious mind that going blind to money would ease your pain. Remove that belief and replace it with a belief more in tune with who you really are. Perhaps your father used the withdrawal of your allowance as a punishment for not doing what he expected. Maybe one or both of your parents tied the acquisition of money to their self-worth. Reflect upon who you are right now and the role you would like money to play in your life going forward. The following exercise introduces you to a tool that might be helpful in rooting out the stories of what money means to you.

---

### EXERCISE 9.2: THE MONEY TIMELINE TOOL

1. On a sheet of paper, or in your journal, draw a straight line from one side of the page to the other. Now label the far-left side "Birth" and the far-right side "Today." Divide the line into seven-year increments. Put a big dot at the point on the line representing age seven and label it "7 Years Old." Mark another big dot and label it "14 Years Old." Continue along the timeline until you reach the end, and label that big dot with today's date.

2. Now remember when you were seven years old. Sit in meditation and picture yourself at that age. See

yourself as you might have been in a school picture or a photograph from a holiday celebration. Sit and breathe in the air—the energy—of being seven. Maybe you had a favorite book or loved a specific game such as jacks or T-ball. Just remember. Think about money. Maybe the tooth fairy left you money. Maybe you received an allowance or money on birthdays and holidays. Remember what it was like to have money at the age of seven. For instance, I remember that half of my birthday money went into my savings account but the other half I could spend. I also remember that there were judgments placed on how I spent my money. My father often asked if I had spent it wisely. There was a certain level of disappointment on his part if I chose to spend my cash on a frivolous item. I am thankful for the lesson in saving money, which has become a lifelong habit. I also have a tendency to be very serious when it comes to spending my "play money." I am sure that some of my father's judgment still resides in my space.

3. Continue with this exercise, remembering what it was like to have money at age fourteen, at twenty-one, and so on until you reach the present time. Journal about your memories. Tap to release the negative energy surrounding your stories. Blow up tons and tons of roses to release other people's thoughts and feelings from your space. You are an adult now; you get to be in charge. Work to clear away the old, and uncover the real you.

In sessions with my clients I have found that the inner critic's voice is particularly loud around issues of money. The technique of tapping, as explained in exercise 2.3, is particularly helpful in rooting out some of the most insidious parts of our internal dialogue. Let's do a little test to bring up the voices of your inner critic and hear what they have to say about the issue of money.

---

### EXERCISE 9.3: THE ONE MILLION DOLLAR TEST

1. Imagine you just won a million dollar lottery. What would you do? Write it down. Think of all the things you could buy, places you would travel, and people you might help. Beside each item on your list, see if you can quantify the cost of that item. For example, if you want to go back to school to earn a degree, estimate the cost of completing your education. If you want to buy a brand-new car, look up the price of that car. Make your list, dream your dreams, and put a price tag next to each item. If you are unsure, just guess at the cost. Enjoy the dreaming. When you have all the items on your list, add up the total.

2. As you were dreaming, you might have heard a voice in your head saying, "You can't have that—it's way too expensive," or one of my favorites, "Who do you think you are? You can't have that! You're not _____ ." (Fill in the blank with whatever foreign energy rings true for you.)

3. Now double the amount of money you have to spend. Go ahead, be brave. See if you can spend another million dollars. As you dream and spend,

tune in to your internal dialogue. The voices might be getting louder and louder as you reach various amounts. Listen to your inner critic as you spend $2 million, then $10 million. What about $100 million?

This is a lesson in examining our boundaries, our set points. At some level, each one of us hits the wall, so to speak, and our internal dialogue—our programming—takes control, limiting our ability to stretch and move to the next level of havingness. Whatever your set point, boundaries are a learned belief and therefore they can be unlearned. You can move beyond your set point into a new territory just by bringing your awareness to the issue and removing the limiting thoughts and feelings.

Perhaps deep down you believe you are unworthy of having gobs of money. Maybe your judgments and internal dialogue about "those rich people" take center stage and you go into serious *less than* mode. Examine the judgments you hold around having money. Look at your money web. Consider whether some of those associations are still true for you. Soon you will work to remove some of those negative beliefs, those stories that are limiting your set point—but for now, journal about what money means to you.

One of the common threads on many money webs is that in order to have money, you have to work hard. For many people, struggle and money go hand in hand. Some of us, those known as workaholics, carry this belief to its extreme. Let's examine this belief.

One of the associations on your web might look something like this:

*Money—work hard—reward-money—*
*happiness—new house—bigger car*

*Work hard—that's what I do—*
*praise—raise—more money*

*Work hard—provide for my family—*
*security—that's my job*

Let's examine this thread and see if the statements hold true in all circumstances. It is sometimes true that if you work hard, you will be rewarded with praise from your boss, and maybe a raise in pay. It is also true that you can work hard and not be rewarded, which often results in resentment and anger.

Money is energy, and as such it flows in and out of our lives. If we continually link working hard with money, then as the tide of money flows out, panic sets in. The inner critic's voice sounds the alarm and we work harder and harder, hoping to bring back the flow of money. But sometimes the flow of money does not return as a result of working harder. The boss might not give us the raise we deserve, or the prospective client chooses not to sign a contract. We've worked hard, but the reward of money never materializes. We blame ourselves for not putting in enough effort, and we dig deeper and work harder, hoping that next time we will get the reward of money. In this vicious cycle, we surround ourselves with the energies of struggle, frustration, resentment, and anger. These are not very inviting energies.

I see money as a light, playful energy. It is almost like a lightning bug buzzing in and out of my life, offering me opportunities and choices. This friendly energy is attracted to energies of the same vibrational family, and I know that panic and resentment are not light and easygoing energies. I may still choose to work hard, but by delinking money from working hard, I stay out of a state of panic and resentment. Instead I choose to work from a state of lightheartedness and ease, knowing that money will flow toward those energies.

## Harnessing the Tool Called Money

Many of the lessons you have explored on this journey of discovery are applicable to the energy of money. You know that your personal template, located in the center of your heart chakra, is a beacon drawing you like a magnet to events and circumstances that are in alignment with the way you see yourself. When you are aligned with your statement of being, powerful waves of energy vibrate out into the world, magnetizing to you events and circumstances that are in alignment with who you are. This beacon calls out, "Hey, come be my friend. Come on over to where the energy is clean and the vibe is cool."

Money is energy, just like thoughts and feelings are. As you grow in your awareness of what money means to you, new messages are being transmitted into the cosmos. Instead of holding the idea that money is dirty, think, "I can have money. I am actually okay now with being rich. I've removed some of that old belief system clogging up my brain, so, Ms. Universe, *please send me more.*"

Like attracts like. As you continue to tune in to these new inner feelings around money, ask yourself, "Am I scared of not having enough money?" Life brings what you ask for, so be clear in your messaging. One of the most important energies to remove from your chakras is that of lack, in all its forms. It's so easy to fall into the story of there being not enough to go around. It's also easy to buy into its corresponding emotion: fear. When you feel fear about your safety and security, your first chakra flares into action, telling the adrenal glands to secrete hormones in an effort to spur your body into defensive action.

To alleviate a fear, you need to remove the underlying belief. In this case, the fear of not being safe and secure is tied to the story that you need money to survive. You may need money to live comfortably, to pay your mortgage, and to send your children to college, but you do not need money to survive. Do the tapping exercise for your story of why you need money to survive. Walk yourself through the scenario of living without money. Maybe you would barter with your neighbors or pool your resources with other community members, allowing each to contribute to the benefit of the whole. See if you conclude that money is a tool and a resource that allows you mobility and ease.

If you remove the fear of a lack of money—if you entertain the notion that money is just a convenient means of exchange and that you can always find another means of ensuring your survival—then you are in control of your thoughts and feelings around the subject of money.

Let's move this energy of money out of your first chakra —your survival space—and up to your third chakra—your power center. With the energy of money residing in your power center, you will be able to harness this force to work for you to help you manifest the life of your dreams.

**EXERCISE 9.4: MOVING YOUR MONEY ENERGY**

1. Close your eyes and be in the center of your head. Breathe, and just be. Check your grounding cord and see your aura filled with your own energy, no one else's. Bring your attention to your first chakra. Now visualize a rose in front of your first chakra. See the rose. Ask the rose to call to it all your feelings and emotions around the scarcity of money. See fear leave your first chakra and head into the rose. Watch as panic, scarcity, and lack enter that rose. Feel into your body, at the base of your spine. Open up that chakra, and allow all foreign energies, all thoughts and feelings that have come to you from your parents or others, to leave this space. Feel all the harsh judgments about how much money is too much leave your space. Once you feel all the emotions calm and the colors diminish, blow up that rose. See it explode in front of you. Feel your first chakra, at the base of your spine, being relaxed and clear.

2. Now let's move the remaining pure money energy— that energy that is yours and no one else's—to its rightful place in the third chakra. See another rose in front of you, and have this rose pull out all the remaining money energy from your first chakra. See the colors as they move into this rose. When the rose is filled, intend for that rose to move from your first chakra to the space in front of your third chakra. See the rose floating around your solar plexus, a little bit higher than your belly button. Now pull that rose into your third chakra. Feel the colors of money

merge with the other energies in your third chakra. This is your power center. Feel a surge of power throughout your body as your third chakra lights up with this added fuel.

3. Know that your money energy is where it belongs and that you have harnessed its power for your use. When you feel complete, open your eyes. Your money energy is now available to fuel your dreams. You may repeat this exercise if you begin to notice thoughts of judgment or panic around money. Money is a neutral tool, that is all.

## Money Mindfulness

If you hate your job and go to work every day filled with dread, that attitude translates to the money you earn from that job. Your paycheck is tinged with that ill will. While not devastating, this situation certainly is not as positive as you may like. Attitude translates to power. Be mindful of how you feel earning your money. Be in a state of ease, be in grace, be happy and in gratitude, even if you work in a job that you do not find satisfactory. Like attracts like. Your state of emotions, your attitude, is a beacon calling to you events that are in alignment with who you are in the present moment. If you want to attract the job of your dreams, then send that message out to the universe. You will learn the technique of creating a mock-up in the next chapter, so consider what you want to manifest.

Understand that how you treat money on a day-to-day basis is the outward expression of your inner money space. Become conscious of how you speak about money. Become aware of your thoughts and feelings around money and what your inner critic has to say on the subject.

If you treat money as you would treat your best friend, then you are sending the message that you appreciate and value money. Like attracts like. Your thoughts and feelings attract other thoughts and feelings of a similar nature. If you want more money in your life, then value it, appreciate it, honor it. As you move into a higher level of consciousness around money, you might want to contemplate how you use money to advance your soul purpose. Money is energy. It is full of potential. As you give, freely and with consciousness, you increase the vibration of the money in your life. Gratitude, love, and appreciation—all those great vibrations—can really increase the level of your prosperity, both internal and external.

## Your Money's Home

The principle I live by is this: How I treat money is the way money will treat me. Place your wallet in front of you. If you've had this particular wallet for some time, it may be dirty or torn. The bills may be crumpled up and sticking out in various directions, along with pieces of paper, sticky notes, bills, and grocery lists. Remembering that money is energy, consider whether your wallet, your money's energetic "home," is inviting. If you were money, would you want to live here?

I treat the money in my wallet like a dear and trusted friend. My money is not crunched up into tiny balls, it is lovingly handled. I straighten out the corners, smooth the bills, turn them so they all face the same way: forward and face up. As I'm doing this, I acknowledge money's importance in my life. I appreciate money, and money appreciates me.

Next, become mindful and respectful of caring for the other places your money calls home. Reconciling your bank statements, keeping tabs on your retirement funds, cleaning out the spare change from your car—all are ways to honor your money. Apply the same organized, caring approach to your credit cards and the larger monetary world that goes beyond the cash in a wallet.

How you treat your money is an indication of how much worth you assign to it. Make a comfortable place for your money to call home—one that's so nice that your money will want to stick around.

## Paying Your Bills in Gratitude

Yes, you heard right. As you pay your bills each month, be in a state of gratitude. You know that your thoughts and emotions radiate from you in waves of energy. Being thankful for the lifestyle you have is an important step in living a life full of grace. By blessing your payments as they leave your space, you are telling the universe that you are grateful for all the experiences those bills represent.

Paying bills in gratitude is as easy as developing a simple blessing as you put a stamp on the envelope or hit the submit button on a retail website. Bless the money that this invoice you're paying represents and the payee for what he or she has given you. Be grateful for the roof over your head as you write out your rent check. Be thankful for the food you eat as you hand over your credit card to the grocery store cashier. Be thankful for all the many ways that money circulates in your life.

## Keep That Money Circulating

The energy of money is much like an ocean wave. It flows in and out, in and out. You receive money for doing something of value, and you give money when you receive something of value. Allowing the flow is an important step in coming to a state of neutrality around the tool called money. It is time to shift your thoughts to prosperity, not lack.

One of the universal laws is that life is a flow of giving and receiving. There is a rhythm, an ebb and flow, to everything. When you are in a state of lack, you are coming from a space of restriction and are inhibiting the flow. The universe always mirrors back to you whatever you do, so become conscious of what you are thinking, feeling, and doing. Consciously create your environment: that is the key.

The universal law of circulation is simple: give what you want to receive. If you want love, give love. If you want more time in your life, then give your time to an organization whose mission is in alignment with your passion. If you want to receive more money, then give money to others.

Give freely, and give from a space of abundance and joy. One way of doing this is to tithe. Tithing is not always religious in nature. Give to an organization that adds to your spiritual growth in some way. It could be that a charity doing important work in your community calls out to you. Or perhaps an organization that offers help to those in need worldwide is something that you wish to support through the energy of money. Tithe in the spirit of freedom and gratitude, with no expectation of receiving something in return from that particular organization.

The amount of your gift is not important; it is the intent that matters. You will receive back the same energy in which you sent your tithe. So be clear of your intent when you write out your check. Be happy, be grateful, and be in a state of appreciation.

Tithing regularly, from a space of gratefulness and plenty, brings you into a state of prosperity. That feeling of ease comes from a knowingness deep within that through the act of giving to others, you are adding light to the planet.

## Creating Your Own Money Story

Now that you have removed from your space other people's stories about what money is, it's time to write your own story. Think about the type of friendship you would like to have with money. Reflect upon how you will use the money tool in your new life—your life on purpose.

Your money story is all about how you feel, your thoughts and emotions about money. Money is neutral; it is just a means of exchanging goods or services with one another. It is a tool residing in your third chakra, your power center, which you utilize to increase your opportunities and mobility.

---

### EXERCISE 9.5: SETTING YOUR MONEY BUBBLE

1. Sit in your meditation space with your eyes closed, feet flat on the floor. Be in the center of your head and just breathe, creating a neutral, present-time vibration in which you can look at the energy of

money. Release your current grounding cord and put on a brand-new one. Make it wide and secure, and set it on maximum release. Allow all foreign energies, all those thoughts of what someone else feels about money, to leave your space and release down your grounding cord. See your aura as clean, clear, and filled with your own energy—no one else's. Get your earth and cosmic energies to flow throughout your body and out the top of your head. Allow yourself to relax and breathe.

2. Intend for a bubble to appear in front of you. See this bubble filled with the colors of your money space. Put a grounding cord on this bubble and drain out any energy that is not yours. Watch as the grounding cord pulls all that foreign energy out of your bubble, leaving it crystal clear.

3. Now fill your bubble with colors representing the qualities that you would like to bring to your awareness of money. Make the bubble as big as you would like. This represents your havingness around money. See the colors of the qualities you associate with money fill the bubble. See the energies flowing, in and out, back and forth. My personal money bubble is big—bigger than my body. I see myself on a rope swing over a river of money. The river is the color of ease, playfulness, choices, and opportunities. As I sway back and forth, I acknowledge that the river below me will always be in motion. In and out, back and forth, high and low, money is a constant flowing energy in my life. As I jump from the swing into the

river, I feel the cool, crisp river of money flow over and through me. I am grateful, appreciative, and at peace as I continue to float downstream.

4. Make your visualization full of images that mean something to you. Maybe you see money gushing from the center of the earth, spewing opportunities and choices. Maybe you see yourself surfing on a wave of money, filling your body with emotions of gratitude and peace.

5. Once you have the bubble exactly as you want it, pull it into your third chakra, your power center. Know that you are intending for money to be a tool that you can harness for your own growth and development.

6. When you feel complete, open your eyes.

My money story has changed over the years. As I've come to terms with my inner critic's voice, I've developed a level of self-confidence and self-worth in all areas of my life. I now know that how I view money is a microcosm of how I view myself. I am worthy. I am worthy of having money, and I am worthy of living a life full of purpose and meaning. So are you.

In the next chapter, we will explore the third key to living your life on purpose: the process of manifesting, or bringing your dreams into physical reality.

### Energy Pointers

- What color (or mixture of colors) is your money energy?

- At the end of your daily meditation, set the intention for your day by thinking, "Today I will be _____ ." (Fill in the blank with a quality such as "focused," "compassionate," or "calm.") Remind yourself of your intention throughout the day.

## Helpful Hints

- Paying money forward is a great way to keep the circulation coming to you. Next time you're at a restaurant, leave your server a generous gift.

- Speak of money as you would a best friend. Listen to your dialogue and choose expansive, open, and relaxed words when you speak about money.

## Chapter 10

# Living on Purpose Key #3: The Process of Manifesting

Living your life on purpose involves more than just thinking positive thoughts, wishing, desiring, and repeating prosperity mantras all day long. Living a life full of purpose and meaning is a process of becoming a conscious creator who intentionally chooses the thoughts, feelings, and beliefs that are in alignment with the life you desire.

When we create something, we always craft its energetic form first as a thought or idea. You might say to yourself, "This year I want to remodel my kitchen." You think the thought and create an image, an energetic blueprint, of your new kitchen. You may picture the new countertops and appliances in your mind and create some sensations around the picture. You may imagine cooking breakfast on your new stove or watching the birds from your kitchen window. These sensory feelings add substance to the thought "I want to remodel my kitchen." As you do this, the thought form grows in power and begins magnetizing to it other energies that are of the same frequency. You might begin to assess whether you can "have" this newly updated kitchen by figuring out costs and discussing it with friends and family. You are now energetically test-driving this desire. If you decide this is a comfortable fit, if you can energetically have it, then your thought form begins to gain physical mass. Maybe you sketch out a design, or you window shop for tile and flooring.

We create our lives this way, thought form to reality, and we do it either consciously or unconsciously. If you had stayed in a dreamy fantasy state about your new kitchen, then the thought form would have attracted more dreamy fantasy energy, and you might never have gotten beyond the wishing and hoping phase. Bringing our awareness and intent to this process of manifesting is our all-important third key to living a life on purpose.

As an example, let's say you want a new car this year. This is not just an idle thought or a fantasy; you've energetically begun the process of test-driving this car. You feel comfortable with the thought "I want a new car." Your budget might be a little thin, but a new vehicle is a reasonable possibility. Most people stop right here in their manifesting process—they haven't consciously looked at the energy state of their desire. But we are different! We understand that the process of bringing life to our dreams is primarily about clearing away any limiting beliefs that may have us stuck in a state of lack. We will use our tools to clear out lack and any other beliefs that may be getting in the way of manifesting our dream life.

In your journal, write out a desire. In our example, the desire is "I want a new car," but the wish could just as easily be "I want to go back to school this year" or "I want to find a beloved." Whatever your desire, write it down.

Now test this desire against any beliefs you hold by examining your current havingness around this desire. First, reassess your belief of whether you can have a new car. When you think the thought "I want a new car," check to see if your stomach drops or you feel a pain in your side. Check in with your inner critic as you say the words aloud, "I want a new car."

- Reflect upon whether you hold a limiting belief around deserving a new car versus a used one. Again, check in with your body and your internal dialogue as you say, "I want a shiny, new, never-before-driven car."

- Picture driving around town in a new car. Check to see if you hold a limiting belief around the judgments the neighbors might have of this bright, shiny, new car.

- Imagine telling your coworkers and boss about the new purchase. If your stomach does a backflip wondering what your boss will say, that's a limiting belief.

Write about how you feel. Examine your beliefs. Know that you can change your belief at any time by consciously choosing a new belief. Use your tools to increase your havingness level to 100 percent. If you have not reached 100 percent havingness yet, then the next exercise will help expand your ability to have this desire and wipe away the last of your limiting beliefs.

---

**EXERCISE 10.1: CLEARING YOUR HAVINGNESS SPACE**

1. Sit in meditation with your eyes closed. Be in the center of your head. Allow yourself a moment to settle down and relax, and take a couple of deep breaths. Ground yourself to the center of the earth. Intend for your chakras to remain neutral, keeping your thoughts and emotions to a minimum.

2. Now imagine a soap bubble in front of you. Ask this bubble to fill with the colors representing your havingness space around that new car. Intend for the bubble to show you whether your fourth chakra (heart center) template and your internal dialogue are a match to having that object, a new car.

3. Imagine the bubble filled with color. If you cannot see it clearly, don't worry; just imagine what it would be like if you could see it. Relax and allow your imagination to flow. You might have a sense of just knowing or imagining colors.

4. Now read the bubble. Consider what the colors mean to you. Each person interprets color in a different way. There is no right or wrong answer, just your answer. For example, let's say your bubble is medium-size, but there are some dense and dull colors in the bubble. There is a tarry-black color with a lot of midnight blue in the center. You also sense there is some buttercup yellow in the background, but it's overshadowed by the darker, denser colors. This

bubble seems smaller than you had imagined. Maybe your havingness level is still not at 100 percent. You may not really believe you deserve a new car. A used car, maybe, but not a brand-new car. The tarry-black color reminds you of resistance, as in "The car may be for someone else, but not for me," whereas the midnight blue reminds you of a should, as in "I shouldn't own a brand-new car." This is not unusual. Even if you have worked your havingness space and done your best to clear out other people's energies from your bubble, you may uncover new clues every time you look. Readings like this are always done in present time, so it's possible that some new foreign energies have managed to take up residence in your bubble.

5. To change the bubble, and thereby change the energetics around your havingness, put a grounding cord on the bubble. Allow this hollow tube to drain out all the resistance and shoulds. Watch as all those colors flow down the grounding cord and leave the space. Once the bubble is drained of all those dark, hard-to-see-through colors, check whether your bubble has changed color. Maybe the buttercup yellow, representing joy, is more dominant now. Imagine filling the bubble with other light or translucent colors, such as those representing excitement, self-worth, and more joy. Watch the bubble fill with those chosen thoughts and colors, and see the bubble grow bigger and fuller. Feel the joy and anticipation fill this bubble until you reach a level of 100 percent havingness.

6. Now take the grounding cord off that bubble. Pull the bubble right into the center of your heart, infusing your aura with a new belief, a new level of havingness. Feel yourself filled with joy, enthusiasm, and self-worth. When you are ready, open your eyes.

Now say aloud, "I want to have a new car." Check to see if your emotions are a little less volatile and your havingness has grown.

## Becoming Clear on What You Want

In his book *Think and Grow Rich*, Napoleon Hill says, "Our brains become magnetized with the dominating thoughts which we hold in our minds, and…these 'magnets' attract to us the forces, the people, the circumstances of life which harmonize with the nature of our dominating thoughts."

No thought is ever lost. Your thoughts leave your aura and are transmitted into the cosmos. They attract back to you thoughts, emotions, events, people, and circumstances that are on the same frequency as the thought that was sent.

This magnet that Hill speaks of works all the time. It works while you are awake and while you are asleep, pulling to you frequencies that are in harmony with your fourth chakra, your heart center. You have thousands of thoughts a day. One minute you might think, "I want a new car," but the next minute you might think, "Wait, maybe I don't want that new car." How do you control your thoughts so that only those that are aligned with your havingness are the magnets?

You don't. You cannot control all your thoughts. There are too many of them. What you can do is become conscious of those thoughts that are limiting and allow them to drift away. Don't give credence to them. Just let them float by. A thought is just a thought. It is nothing until you attach a story to it.

Use the techniques discussed at the beginning of this book to help assess or dispel your destructive thoughts. Pull those thoughts out of your head and put them into a rose, then blow up that rose. Use the tapping technique to quell a story that no longer suits you. Decide to make friends with your internal dialogue and understand the underlying message. Know that random thoughts will not dislodge a conscious belief, unless you allow it to happen.

To limit the potential of a random thought interfering with your belief that you can have a new car, become clear about what you want. Describe your new car. Maybe you want a four-wheel-drive vehicle that seats at least six people. Or maybe you would like a sports car, all shiny and new, with leather seats and a high-horsepower engine with that wonderful throaty sound.

Can't decide between the two? Well, if you can't decide, then the universe isn't going to decide for you. The universe will throw up its hands and say, "Geez, make up your mind, will you? I'd be happy to give you what you ask for, but I gotta know what that is!"

It is the multiple requests that you send out, either consciously or unconsciously, that get in the way of manifesting what you desire. So get clear. Write it down. Make a list of what is important. If the color of that new car is not that important, leave it out of the request. Give the universe something to work with. Avoid random thoughts as you focus on what you want to manifest.

Once you are clear about what you want, then visualize the car in front of you. If you decided on the sports car, then see it. Imagine the smell of the leather seats. See yourself sitting in the driver's seat, with one hand on the wheel and the other on the gearshift. Feel your left foot push down on the clutch while your right hand shifts gears. Feel the car move into another gear as it accelerates down the road.

Feelings are important. Make this desire as real as you can. The belief that you can have a new car is fueled by your thoughts and feelings. So write it out. Spend time making your thoughts and feelings crisp, clean, and clear. Say your desire aloud to yourself. Feel it. Be it. Know that as you do, you are adding fuel to your manifestation project.

Sometimes no matter how much you desire something, no matter how well you work with the law of attraction, things do not turn out the way you planned. Let's say that instead of manifesting a new car, you want to manifest a new job. Your current position has you tied in knots because you and your boss are not getting along. You want out. In your visualization, you see yourself free and joyful, sitting at a new desk happily working away. You can taste it and feel it, and so you are certain that this is the manifestation for you.

Wait! What if one of your life lessons is to learn to speak clearly and come from your heart in difficult conversations? Maybe your current job, with your I-am-having-trouble-relating-to-you boss, is providing you with the opportunity to learn to speak clearly and state what you desire.

All of us come to this planet with a core lesson or two that we have chosen to deal with in this lifetime. If you move to another job before you clear this lesson, you will find that the lesson follows you to your new job. Soon your new job will be no different from the old job. You will be miserable all over again.

Pull out your statement of being. Read it aloud. Now imagine the item you are going to manifest. Check to see if it fits within your statement of being. Maybe a new car is neutral—neither in alignment nor out of alignment with your statement of being. It could be that both jobs are in alignment; it's just the relationship with your current boss that is off-kilter. Pause and consider. It may be that what you want to manifest is just a way of running away from something. Make sure that what you want to manifest is in alignment with your internal Spirit and is not just a diversion from a life lesson.

Gulp! If you find that it is a life-lesson situation, then work on that lesson first. You may find that you do not need to manifest a new job. The old job is just fine once you have learned to communicate clearly and state your truth in a state of neutrality and amusement.

## The Chakras and Manifesting

Let's move on to the next step in the manifestation process. You have aligned your manifestation project with your statement of being. Either it is neutral to your growth, as in the case of a new car, or it actually enhances your growth and moves you up the ladder of life lessons. Your thoughts are clear about what you want, and your emotions are in alignment with your desire. You know you can have it, yet you are not grasping after, nor striving toward, your car. Your hands are cupped, waiting to receive.

You are almost there. There's one more factor that needs consideration. Each chakra has a part to play in manifesting what you want. If your chakras are full of other people's energies, then you might be manifesting the life of someone else's dreams. If you live a life that is similar to your sibling's, or if you drive the same type of car as a neighbor, it may be that their energy is in your space, in your chakras, and blinding you to thoughts of your own.

### The First Chakra: Survival

Located at the base of your spine, the first chakra is the primal chakra. It is the seat of survival: food, water, and shelter are the main concerns of this chakra. The glands associated with the first chakra are the adrenals.

Look around at your home, the food in your refrigerator, the town where you live. See the positive. You have a roof over your head, you have food to eat, and you probably have a car to drive around town. You are a powerful being. Look at what you have already unconsciously manifested. So often we notice only the negatives, but for now, check out the positives. See all that you have attracted into your life. You can certainly have more, but take a moment to see it, feel it, touch it. Be in gratitude for your life, the life in which all your first-chakra needs are being met.

This state of conscious appreciation for what you have allows you to get rid of negativity, the thoughts of lack, the feelings of powerlessness. Being in a state of appreciation allows you to become neutral to your manifestation. If you manifest that new car, you will feel great. You will jump up and down with joy and excitement, but you will not die if you do not get it. That is being neutral. It is understanding that yes, this new car will enhance your life, but you can survive without it. That level of non-attachment is important. It allows the manifestation to rest in a place of abundance, not lack. It is like saying, "You know, I would love a new car, and I know that I can have a new car, and I'm also okay *not* having a new car because I already live in abundance. I can see all that I have manifested in my life, and I am so grateful." For all that you have in your life, be in gratitude and acceptance.

### The Second Chakra: Seat of Emotions

Non-attachment means that while you desire the object you are working to consciously manifest, you are in a space of neutrality around the desire. Your second chakra is the seat of desires, feelings, and emotions—and too much desire can lead to poor results. A state of grasping, craving, striving, and reaching is actually detrimental to achieving what you desire because you are coming from a state of lack. You grasp at something you do not have. You crave something you are missing. Instead, you could acknowledge that this new car would be great to have but your world will not fall apart if you have to drive your current car for another year. Sure, it would be lovely to have a new car, but your emotions are under control, and you are neutral to the need.

Let's test this out. Bring to mind your manifestation project. Then tune in to your body as you read these statements out loud:

- I really, really, really want this.
- I don't know what I'll do if this manifestation doesn't materialize.
- I must have this!

If you felt your stomach clench or your throat constrict as you read these statements, then you still might have some foreign energy in your aura around the need or craving. Spend some time cleaning out your first and second chakras. You could practice stomping out the energy or blowing up a rose. Live in certainty that you may have whatever you want to manifest.

### The Third and Fourth Chakras: Power and Affinity

Your third chakra is your power center. This chakra is your center of personal fuel that will power your desire into reality. If this chakra is full of shoulds and other people's energies, then your manifestation project may be a way to compensate for a lack of internal validation. Check to see if your desire is based upon a need to gain someone's approval or to balance a feeling of inadequacy.

Your fourth chakra is your affinity center. This is your beacon, calling to you events, people, and circumstances that are in alignment with your personal template. Ask yourself whether your self-worth is tied to the event or circumstance that you want to manifest.

Notice how your stomach and heart react when you think the following thoughts:

- I really, really, really want this.
- I don't know what I'll do if this manifestation doesn't materialize.
- I must have this!

Decide if you are straining after something because other people say you should have this or do that. Consider whether your neighbor or boss just acquired something similar to your manifestation project. Are you envious? Put out a bubble and check the energy of your third and fourth chakras. Be neutral and remove any thoughts and feelings of lack.

### *The Fifth Chakra: Communication*

Your fifth chakra is your communication center. Let's do a test on how you communicate about your manifestation project. Tell your neighbor, your coworker, or your best friend about your desire. Listen to your language as you describe the car that you want to manifest, or the move you want to make to a different city. Notice what words you are using. Notice if you are having trouble articulating exactly what you want to manifest. Notice if the words are stuck in your throat or if you feel a tightness in your stomach as you explain that you are not happy with what you have and that you want more.

This exercise is not about what your neighbor says to you when you explain that you want a new car; this is about your ability to get the words out of your mouth.

Check to see whether you can "have" this new car. Check in with the emotions in your body and the thoughts going through your head as you communicate your desire. Make sure that you are clear within yourself about this desire. And before you begin, you might want to place a protective bubble around your aura to catch any envy or jealousy your neighbor may throw your way.

### The Sixth and Seventh Chakras: Seeing the World and the Divine

Your sixth chakra is all about how you see the world. Check to see if you are viewing your desire through the lens of craving or grasping. Notice if you are striving after your dream because you believe that there is only so much to go around and you had better get your fair share before it's all gone.

Your seventh chakra is your connection to the Divine. As you sit in meditation, ask yourself whether your manifestation project is in alignment with your Highest and Best Self. Read your statement of being aloud as you ask for guidance.

Be in a state of neutrality. Imagine all seven chakras vibrating in quiet anticipation. Fill your aura with the energy of realistic excitement.

## Manifesting What You Desire

You are comfortable with your ability to have a new car this year. You can picture it, you can smell that new-car smell, and you can see yourself driving down the highway in it. The color is a bright cherry red, and you've chosen a convertible. You don't care about the make and model, but it must have leather seats and a manual transmission.

You are also in a relaxed space about this car. Yes, it would be great to have it, but you do not need it. You can live without it. Your desire is there, but it is not a craving. Your self-worth is not tied to this car; you will be the same with or without it. When you speak about the car, your words, while full of excitement and joy, are neutral, coming from a place of neither lack nor overt desiring. You are clear that this car is in affinity with who you are right now, and you are feeling a sense of certainty concerning this want.

So let's move on to the actual process of making this desire a reality by creating what I call a *mock-up*. A mock-up is the energetic prototype or template of the physical object you desire. Instead of just wishing and hoping that life will go our way, there's a way to consciously create the life of our dreams. This technique involves visualizing in detail what we want to create and then asking the universe to bring it into our physical world.

---

### EXERCISE 10.2: CREATING A MOCK-UP

1. Sit in a comfortable chair, feet flat on the floor. Close your eyes and take a couple of deep breaths. Be in the center of your head, free of all distractions, and feeling relaxed, comfortable, and in command of

your surroundings. Ground yourself, set your aura at a color of your choosing, and see your protection bubble encasing your aura. Run your earth and cosmic energies, and intend for your body and aura to be set to a neutral vibration.

2. Now, out in front of you, imagine a soap bubble. This is your mock-up bubble. Put a grounding cord on the bubble and watch it fill with colors. See the heavy colors drain away, and watch the bubble stabilize in front of you. Iridescent colors fill it. Pick colors that represent certainty, knowingness, and self-worthiness to you. You can "have" this bubble and you can "have" this mock-up.

3. Now fill your mock-up bubble with pictures and feelings representing the item or event you would like to mock up. Make it real. See the colors, smell the smells, and see the energies and pictures develop before your eyes. When you have the bubble filled with exactly what you want, imagine a gold beam of energy, representing the Divine, coming down from the cosmos and kissing the top of your bubble of energy. Write the words "or something better" across the top of your bubble. Say, "I know this mock-up will come to me by divine right, in perfect timing, with ease and grace." Untether the bubble and shoot it off into the universe. Open your eyes and come out of meditation.

You have taken a thought and a feeling—your mock-up—scrubbed away all lack and worry, and set that thought and feeling in the vibration of clarity and certainty. You have acknowledged that the mock-up is in alignment with your statement of being and your Highest Self, asked for divine guidance, and then sent that thought and feeling off to become a physical item or event. You are now waiting in ease and grace for your thought and feeling, in the tangible form of your mock-up, to return to you.

It is better to separately mock up each item or event that you desire. This lesson came home to me when I first began experimenting with mock-ups. I had about five things that I wanted to mock up one year, and I was impatient. I had other things occupying my mind, so I mocked up all five things at one time. I created one huge mock-up bubble filled with colors and feelings representing my five desires.

One of those desires was to spend part of the winter in a warmer climate and another was to sell my current residence and move into a small cottage in the same city. I even went so far as to describe, in detail, the little white cottage. I pictured a long driveway to the right of the house, culminating in a detached garage that sat back from the street. The cottage was white, and I could see the fireplace brick on the exterior of the house as I drove in the long drive. I sent out lots and lots of information, and guess what I manifested? My residence never sold, so the white cottage never came into my reality. *But*...I vacationed in a sweet, white cottage located in a warmer climate, with a long drive along the right side of the house. The house (it was a little bit bigger than a cottage) even had exposed exterior fireplace brick that could be seen as you came up the long drive.

Yes, I got what I asked for. My mock-up certainly came in, but it came to me in a way I had not expected. The moral of the story is to be clear about what you ask for and mock up only one desire up at a time. *You really do get what you ask for.*

## Helpful Hints for Manifesting Mock-Ups

- You do not need to know how the manifestation will come into your life. The mechanics of how your budget will stretch are not the point of the process. Just do the mock-up and be surprised by the how. You might receive an unexpected raise or bonus at work and spend it on remodeling your kitchen. Maybe your best friend will introduce you to the person who becomes your life partner. You never know! There are all kinds of ways that your manifestation can show up, so do not set limits, and allow surprises.

- You cannot just sit at home wishing and hoping for a dream to be fulfilled. You must bring your intention and awareness to your desire. Set your intention, shout that message to the edges of the earth, and sit in certainty that it is coming your way. Then do the legwork. If you want a new job, update your résumé, network, and apply for job postings. If you want a new bedroom set, check out the furniture stores in your area and online, preparing for the day you will actually pay for and have the furniture delivered.

- Do not mock up money just to have money. Money is a tool; it flows like a river, in and out of your life. Mock up what you want to do with money. The money will be there to allow you to have your mock-up. Remember that feelings are the key to a successful mock-up. Think about your feelings around having money. Now think about your feelings around having a home. Feel the difference? The universe can feel the difference too. Mock up your dream, and the money will follow.

- If you mock up a fantasy, you will be given a fantasy. In other words, base your mock-up in reality. Take it a step at a time. If you want to take a trip around the world, then be specific. Write down the countries you want to visit and the sites you want to see. Make it real, and the cosmos will respond. Mock up a trip without specifics, and the universe may bring you a dream about a trip around the world. Know the difference.

- Only mock up your desire once. This one is a hard one. Often we send out unconscious thoughts about what we want to be, do, or have. If you've ever stood in front of a store window, gazing at a new pair of shoes, and thought, "I want those," that is an unconscious mock-up. Maybe the next day you look down at your friend's feet and see another pair of shoes that you love, and you think to yourself, "I want those shoes instead!" You now have two unconscious mock-ups out there, competing with each other and wiping out the potential of actually moving your dream shoes into your reality.

As you wait in certainty for your mock-up to come, work on your havingness space. It really is all about how you feel and whether you allow yourself the feeling of havingness. Check in to see if you feel unworthy or lacking in any way. An example would be wondering about the how. Remember to allow for flexibility in the execution of this mock-up. If you find yourself second-guessing, redoing, or adding more to your mock-up—stop! Relax and be in certainty. Put all those negative feelings and thoughts of lack into a rose and blow up the rose.

## Mocking Up Your Own Parking Karma

While you're waiting for your mock-up to come in, let's try another simple mock-up that will add some amusement to your day.

A friend of mine has the best "luck" in finding great parking spaces. Every time a group of us goes out for lunch, we ask Laurel to drive because she always finds a parking space right in front of the restaurant. How does she do it? She is in certainty. She knows, with all of her being, down to the tips of her toes, that there is an empty parking space with her name on it, just waiting for her to appear. Over the years, Laurel has had many experiences of driving into a parking lot just as the car in front of her was leaving a prime space. Now she just expects it. She intuitively knows that she will find a great place to park her car. She just knows it. She is certain. Therefore she does.

Be in this certainty about your mock-up. Visualize it coming to you. Know with every fiber of your being that it is yours. Just know, and it will be.

Try mocking up some parking karma of your own. As you get in your car to run some errands, sit in meditation for a moment. While you are buckling yourself in, ground yourself and your car. That is always a great idea. Next, see a mock-up bubble in front of you, ground it, and set the intention that the bubble will fill with the colors of certainty. Visualize an open parking space right where you want it, when you want it. Be in certainty. See a golden light surround your mock-up bubble, then unground the bubble and shoot it to the edge of the planet. Open your eyes, come out of meditation, and know that good parking spaces are yours to have.

### Energy Pointers

- What color is your havingness energy today?
- Become conscious of your unconscious mock-ups.

### Helpful Hints

- If you catch yourself unconsciously mocking up the same thing in numerous ways, then just ask the universe for a do-over. Consciously call back all the old mock-ups, blow them up, then start over. The universe will understand.
- Parking karma mock-ups really do work.

## Chapter 11

# Living on Purpose Key #4: Mindfulness

You have sent the mock-up of your new car, home, or desire out into the world. You know that it will come to you at the perfect time, in ease and grace. You are certain. You just have to wait. And that's the rub: waiting. Not checking in on your mock-up and not reordering it, but just waiting in a state of quiet anticipation. Of course you still do the legwork of sending out résumés or preplanning your move, but you do so with an attitude of confidence and trust. This is the fourth and final key to living your life on purpose: waiting in certainty.

Waiting is not anticipating what is to come, nor is it wondering if your mock-up was done correctly. Waiting in certainty is living in the present moment, being mindful of where you are right now. Waiting is neither past nor present, it's NOW—in big capital letters. You may have heard about mindfulness and even tried it to some degree in your life. You may have become confused about what constitutes "present moment" or just given up because your mind kept wandering to your to-do list or a future event.

Mindfulness is being present with your thoughts and feelings in the current moment. It is being aware of your body, your thoughts, your feelings, the sensations, the smells, and the noises, yet not being distracted by them or judging them. It's not as easy as it sounds, as you'll see in the following exercise.

---

### EXERCISE 11.1: MINDFULNESS EXPERIENCE

1. As you read this page, notice your body. Read the words and feel the sensations in your arms, your legs, your eyes. Right now, that is all. Just feel the sensations and keep reading.

2. Feel your eyes move across the page. Check to see if you are restless as you try to do two things at once, paying attention to the written words on this page and the sensations in your body. Maybe you become distracted by the sensations around you and miss a few words of text.

Mindfulness is a skill, like learning to ride a bike. Thankfully, you have already acquired some training wheels: what I call the center of the head. When you are in the center of your head and present in your body, you are in the present moment. Your thoughts, your feelings, and your intuition are all emanating from one spot: the center of your head. You are in present time, acting with full potency. Your energy is not scattered in the past, nor is it over in a friend's aura or rethinking your most current mock-up. You are in your body, and your Spirit is in the driver's seat. Coming from this space of awareness, you are able to discern your thoughts from those of your neighbor. You are able to feel into your body and sense whether a feeling is truly aligned with your Spirit. You are present.

---

**EXERCISE 11.2: FIVE MINUTES OF MINDFULNESS**

Take five minutes to sit and breathe. Turn off the TV, turn off the phone, turn away from your computer. Turn away from your outside life and go within. Set a timer for five minutes from now, and just sit and observe your thoughts. Can you do it?

1. Sit in a comfortable chair, with your feet on the floor. Close your eyes and breathe. Bring all of your awareness to the center of your head. Imagine sitting as a Spirit in your internal sanctuary, that space between the ears and behind the eyes. Be there now.

2. Count your breaths: in, out, in, out. Breathe and be present. As thoughts enter your mind, which they will, allow them to float by. Breathe. Feel the rhythm of your body as it breathes. Feel your mind slow down as it tunes in to the rhythm of the in-breath and the out-breath. Feel your body: the sensations of breathing, the muscles in your body relaxing, the eyelids drooping. Feel. Be. Do nothing, be everything. That is all.

3. Remain totally present in this moment. If a thought of the future or the past comes up, just say, "Thanks—I'll

be with you in a moment," and go back to breathing and counting your breaths.

4. Feel the tempo of your body and your thoughts. Be fully here, fully present in the moment.

5. Open your eyes and look around the room. See it as if for the first time. Experience the colors, the way the light shines on the table. This is your present moment.

6. Breathe. That is it: just breathe and observe. Feel. Be. Do not judge. Do not listen to the inner critic. Just keep breathing and looking around and feeling and being.

7. Before you jump back into your life, consider how you felt and what you observed during this five-minute mindfulness break. If you enjoyed the sensations, the ease, and the relaxation, then do this again and again. Over and over. Soon it will become part of your normal way of being.

## Living with No Regrets

I had tea with a couple of friends not long ago, and we talked about mindfulness and what it means to be in the present moment. My friend Nancy lives each moment of her life with no regrets. At that particular moment, she was enjoying our friendship and the tea. She was present with our conversation, not worrying about her upcoming meeting or the day's to-do list. She said everything she wanted to say, leaving nothing out, not censoring her thoughts or comments as we conversed. Then, when she departed, she left us totally, moving on to the next thing in her day. Nancy did not carry with her the "coulda, woulda, shoulda" from our conversation. She left it all right on the table when she left.

This is such a vivid description of mindfulness and living your life on purpose. Energetically, Nancy was totally in her body, in the center of her head, operating at full potency. She was comfortable enough in her own skin that she could say what she needed to say irrespective of her inner critic. Her fifth chakra (communication) was open and clear, allowing her to express herself fully. And then, when that moment was complete, she moved on. Just like that. No regrets.

## Practicing Nonjudgment

Living life with no regrets is staying in the vibration of grace. Grace is being complete within yourself. You are not looking outside for validation; you know that you are fine just the way you are. You have calmed your inner critic, and the voices of internal judgment have quieted. You may be better now at not judging yourself, but what about other people?

When you stand in judgment of another person, you send out a vibration of nonacceptance. You do not see other people as they are, right now, in present time. Instead, you hold an expectation, a judgment, of how they should be, what they should say, and how they should react. In addition, when they do not live up to your expectations, you judge them as being wrong, uncaring, or as not holding your same values. You invalidate them. Instead of seeing them for who they really are, you see them as you think they should be.

You know what that energy feels like. When someone throws invalidation energy your way, it reduces you, making you feel small and unworthy. In this journey of discovery, you have learned that the type of energy you send out into the world is reflected back to you, just like a boomerang. If you send out judgmental energy, you will get judgment thrown back in your direction. If you are surrounded with your own internal dialogue of invalidation, criticism, and self-judgment, you will attract more of that energy into your space.

Loving yourself for who you are right now is the key. As you treat yourself, so will other people treat you. If you accept yourself for who you are right here, right now, then you stand in a vibration of nonjudgment. Holding the thought of compassion, for others and yourself, you allow people to be who they are without expectation. That is living a life from a state of mindfulness.

---

**EXERCISE 11.3: DEFLECTING ANGER AND JUDGMENT**

Standing in the vibration of nonjudgment requires repetition and patience. It's difficult to remain mindful during a stressful discussion or argument. With practice, you will remember to pause, be in the center of your head, ground, and remain neutral. Practice remaining fully present—in the center of your head—the next time you feel some expectation energy coming your way.

1. When you are speaking with a person who is angry or judgmental, pause and be aware of your aura. Cover your aura with a protective bubble of your

choice. Maybe you choose to put a glass wall around your aura, or maybe you imagine a mesh covering that surrounds your aura. Watch as these protective devices prevent criticism and harsh judgment energy from entering your aura.

2. As the judgmental person is speaking, watch the energy of their words come in contact with your aura, but without penetrating it. Stand in mindfulness, fully present, without resistance, and just watch as your protection bubble does its job. Stay neutral and just watch. You might not even hear what the other person is saying because you are so engrossed in watching the colors of the words drop away from your space. Yes, words have colors.

3. See what you see, notice what you notice, and be aware of the energies of criticism and judgment bypassing your aura. Just watch and be in nonjudgment.

4. As you do so, notice that in this state of being mindfully aware, you may not feel the need to engage in rhetorical comments. You are standing back and, from your observer space, feel less of a need to throw expectation and harsh judgment energy of your own.

## Forgiveness: For Giving Space

Mindfulness is learning to accept yourself and others exactly as they are with compassion and grace. As you release all judgments and expectations, you enter the vibration of forgiveness: *for giving space.* You learn to give yourself, and those around you, some room to grow, some room to be just the way they are, right now, in this moment. In this space of forgiveness, you are not condoning another's behavior, nor are you judging the whats or the whys. You are allowing it to be, that's all.

Being in this space of forgiveness is one of the hardest lessons to learn. It requires you to look at your world with gentleness, patience, and understanding. You do this as you enter the vibration of accepting all that is. Compassion is a very high vibration, full of kindness, understanding, and patience. Here, you stand apart from value statements, judgments, condemnations, and expectations. You give space to those around you to be, just as they are, right here and right now. Moreover, you give space to yourself to be just who you are in this moment.

Think of someone who stirs up lots of emotions and feelings for you. This individual may be one of your primary mirrors. You have tapped and tapped and tapped about events and memories associated with this person, yet there is still more. You may be in the midst of an internal battle, knowing that you are throwing expectation and judgment at this person but finding yourself unable to step away from the drama. You want to give this person space to be exactly who they are, but there's a lot of resistance energy running through your body.

Remember that forgiveness is about giving space to the other person as well as to yourself. It is not about condoning behavior, it is about acceptance—that is all. Ask yourself whether you are ready to make some headway—any headway—in clearing the air between you and the other person. If not, that's fine. You can return to this meditation another time. If you are ready to take a step toward forgiveness, then continue on with the following meditation.

The origins of this meditation are difficult to trace. Many cultures around the world have used similar techniques to remove resistance and come into a state of forgiveness—a state of grace. I was given this information by a friend who had acquired the information from a friend of hers. That's the way it works. We are given wisdom when we need it the most, and sometimes in rather roundabout ways.

Most world religions include teachings on the nature of forgiveness, and many of these teachings are handed down from person to person without thought to ownership or provenance. Blue is often considered the color of clear communication, and a blue room is often used in meditative practices as a place of calm and peace. Together, these pieces form the basis for the following meditation that I offer to you.

---

### EXERCISE 11.4: THE BLUE ROOM MEDITATION
### OF FORGIVENESS

1. Sit in a comfortable chair in a room where you will not be disturbed. Keep your feet flat on the floor, with eyes closed, and breathe. Take some deep, cleansing breaths, and bring all of your awareness to the center of your head. Be there now.

2. Release your current grounding cord, placing a new one around your hips. Feel it sink into the center of the earth. Set your grounding cord on maximum release, and feel your body sink a little bit deeper

into your chair. See your aura tucked into your
grounding cord.

3. Bring your awareness to the energy leaving your
aura. See it draining out the grounding cord. Feel
yourself filled with your own energy, clean and clear.
Put a protection bubble around your aura, and ask
for this covering to deflect any foreign energy
heading your way.

4. Intend for some earth energy to enter the soles of
your feet, travel up your legs and thighs, enter the
front of your first chakra, and cascade like a waterfall out the back of your first chakra and down your
grounding cord. Notice the color of your earth
energy. Feel its neutral vibration calm your body
and mind.

5. Now see some cosmic energy entering the top of
your crown and flowing down your neck and back.
Feel this energy enter the back of your first chakra.
Watch as the mixture of earth and cosmic energies
moves up the front of your body, through your belly,
up your chest, and through your face, ultimately
spouting out of the top of your head like water.
Feel this mixture of earth and cosmic energies swirl
through your aura, bringing neutral energy to all
parts of your system. See some of this mixture branch
off at your throat, traveling down your arms, to spout
out your palms.

6. Sit in this state of relaxed awareness for a moment
or two. Now visualize a golden sun above your head.
See a magnet in this sun. Ask for the magnet to draw

to it any of your energy, your life force, that you have left scattered in past conversations or future events. Feel these missing parts of you zoom back into the sun, where they will be refreshed and brought to a vibrational frequency that is just right for your body. Fill this sun with the energy of clarity of thought, compassion, wisdom, and any other energy you would like to bring into your body right at the present moment. Pop the golden sun and fill in with the energy. Feel all this golden sun energy enter the top of your head and course through your body, all the way down to the tips of your toes. Feel this shimmering light spread from your body to your aura, filling you to the brim. Feel yourself fully present and vibrating in the energies of peace, clarity of thought, and grace.

7. Bathe your throat chakra in sky-blue energy, intending this energy to open your throat and allow you to communicate all your thoughts and emotions completely and clearly.

8. Imagine yourself seated in a room filled with this same expansive blue energy. The walls are blue, the floor is blue, and the air surrounding you is tinted blue. You are sitting in one chair, and there is another chair directly across from you. See that chair. Notice any sensations that arise in your body. Acknowledge those sensations, breathe, and intend to remain in a calm, neutral vibration.

9. The person you would like to forgive will soon occupy that empty chair. Notice any feelings of

resentment or stories about the hurts and humilia-
tions that arise in your body. Stop for a moment
and ask those feelings to leave your aura. See them
draining out into a rose. When the emotions have all
moved over to the rose, blow it up. Feel calm, clear,
and ready to move on. If you need to blow up some
more roses, do so now. Take as long as you need to
clear the emotions and return to a neutral state of
being.

10. When you are ready, see the person come into this
blue room and sit across from you in the empty
chair. See that person. Notice if they feel a little
apprehensive or scared. Maybe they hesitate before
taking the seat. Maybe there's a scowl on their face
or their fists are clenched.

11. Notice how you feel as you watch this person. If
you observe some sensations arising in your body,
then stop and assess them. Imagine those thoughts,
feelings, and sensations draining down your grounding cord. Intend for your body to be relaxed and for
the words to flow easily from your throat.

12. Now speak to this person about what is on your
mind. Say it all. Tell them how you feel. Feel
yourself communicating every single bit of information that you want to share. They will be able to
respond in a moment, but for now, the floor is all
yours. Say it all. Get it out.

13. If, by chance, you are ready to forgive this person
and are ready to allow them to be just as they are
right now, then repeat the following phrases aloud:

- *I forgive myself, and I forgive you, (person's name), for any past wrongdoings and words said in haste or with malice.*

- *I forgive myself, and I forgive you, (person's name), for any and all hurts.*

- *I look at myself, and I look at you, (person's name), with eyes full of compassion and understanding.*

- *I value myself, with all my quirks and idiosyncrasies, and I value you, (person's name), with all your quirks and idiosyncrasies.*

- *I give myself space to be who I was meant to be, and I give you, (person's name), space to be who you were meant to be.*

- *I love myself, and I love you, (person's name).*

14. After repeating these phrases, allow the other person a chance to speak. Hear all that they have to say to you. Maybe they will share something that will surprise you.

15. When you feel complete, see the other person rise from the chair and leave the room. Sit for a moment in silence and feel this blue room filled with compassion and grace. When you are ready, leave the blue room, returning to the center of your head. Allow yourself a moment or two of validation. Fill in with another golden sun. Then open your eyes and come out of meditation.

For giving space. Allowance. Nonjudgment. Compassion. Grace. The thoughts and feelings you send out into the world are traceable to circumstances in your life. Be a beacon of kindness and gentleness. How you treat others is how others will treat you. Give others the space to be, and they will give you the space to be who you really are.

As we head into the final leg of our journey together, reflect upon the energy surrounding you. Become aware of whether your inner critic's voice has been replaced with the voice of your own inner wisdom. Notice whether you are able to stand in your own truth, not the truth of others. Observe how you relate to yourself and others and how much more expansive your aura has become. You are shining for all to see. We will put the pieces together soon, but for now, bask in the knowledge that you are a being of Light, here to express your uniqueness by living your life on purpose.

### Energy Pointers

- Colors that you can't see through are foreign—they appear dark and pasty. Colors that are translucent, that you can see through, are yours.

- What you resist persists. Become aware of resistance by asking yourself the following question: "What would it be like if I stopped fighting this and just accepted my current situation?"

### Helpful Hints

- Take a mindfulness break during the day. Next time you are waiting in line, pause, look around, see the people surrounding you, and send beacons of grate-fulness from your heart chakra to theirs.

- Pay attention to your aura. This is your home. Fill your aura with energies you are proud of.

## Chapter 12

# Discovering Your True North

As we begin the final part of our work together in this book, let's look back on how far we have traveled on this journey of discovery. We know that thoughts and feelings are forms of energy that radiate throughout the cosmos. Everyone sends out energy and receives energy—all day, every day. As you have integrated this awareness, you have reevaluated the quality of your deepest thoughts and feelings. You know, deep within your being, that what you think and feel you will be. Everything in your life—your relationships, your job, your home—is the product of your thoughts and feelings. You create your reality from the inside out. Life does not just happen to you; you create it by magnetizing to you events and circumstances that are in alignment with your current belief system.

Be grateful for all the wonderful experiences in your life. You created them. Moreover, be grateful for the less-than-ideal parts. Yes, you created those too. Take responsibility for everything: the good, the not-so-good, and even the downright ugly aspects of your life. Be in gratitude for this present moment in time. By shifting your basic assumptions and beliefs so that you bring them into alignment with your statement of being, you are transforming your life.

Your aura and your chakras are the storehouse of thoughts and feelings, yours and everyone else's. When you are living a life full of joy, gratitude, love, and happiness, you are clear of other people's thoughts, feelings, and expectations. You are able to hear your own inner voice, your Spirit, speak to you.

The whispers of Spirit may have grown in volume on this journey. Your statement of being is your Spirit speaking directly to you, challenging you to live a life full of meaning and purpose.

Your personal magnetic template is in place, beckoning like-minded energies your way. Your havingness space and your money space are clear, allowing you to be bigger and grander than you ever imagined.

You have learned how to do a mock-up to send desires out to the universe, knowing that they will be returned to you at the perfect time, with ease and grace. And you've learned to wait in certainty—to be in the here and now, not chasing your dreams or regretting your past. You know how to be fully present, waiting with cupped hands for the universe to answer your requests for new cars, new homes, and anything else you want. But what about the larger purpose, your *life purpose?* Let's ask the universe and your Spirit to help you uncover the path to your own true north.

## Clearing the Shoulds

Just saying the words "life purpose" may bring some emotions to the surface. These emotions are attached to the shoulds of life, as in "I should know what my purpose is. Life is short, and unless I think seriously about why I am alive, I will have wasted my time here on Earth." On the other hand, you may be thinking, "My family tells me that I should become a doctor, a lawyer, or at least a productive member of society. But all I want to do is have fun and play."

Somewhere along the line, you may have been taught that life is serious business, full of angst and inner strife. I think by now you realize that these expectations are other people's thoughts and feelings about who you should be and what you should do. Of course, your family and friends have your best interests at heart, but they do not know your true purpose; they are just projecting onto you their hopes and fears. You have tools now to recognize this energy for what it is. You do not need to accept the expectations of others. You can tune in to, and draw strength from, your own inner wisdom.

Removing the should statements is a necessary precursor to discovering your life purpose. Here is an exercise that might be helpful.

---

**EXERCISE 12.1: LISTING YOUR SHOULDS**

1. Sit in meditation and intend for all the should statements about your life purpose to float to the surface. Come out of meditation and start writing

them down. Do not edit your work. Just write and write and write.

2. If you are stuck, return to meditation and breathe. Just relax and ask that the words and phrases come to your mind representing what people have said you should do with your life. Then write some more. Get those shoulds out of your head.

3. Find at least a hundred phrases representing what other people have said you should be, what your life purpose should be. As an example, here is a partial list that might get your creative juices flowing.

My life purpose is:

- to be happy.
- to find a job that I love.
- to put the other person first, always.
- to heal those around me.
- to leave a legacy, letting others know that I was here, that I mattered.
- to bring people of diverse backgrounds together.
- to have children.
- to get a high-paying job that will bring immense satisfaction.
- to live close to my family and take care of them.
- to play more.
- to play less.

- to be kinder.
- to be softer.

   If you are stuck, try changing the phrase to *I am
   expected to be* _____.

4. As emotions surface, tap on your meridian points,
   blow up some roses, and remove the energy of the
   shoulds of your life purpose. You are here to do great
   things, yes, but you are also here to live a life of joy
   and happiness in ease and grace.

## Listening to Your Inner Wisdom

Your life purpose may be something so familiar that you fail
to recognize it. So let's go on a treasure hunt to find clues to
your uniqueness, your internal voice. This is not a difficult
task, because the clues are right under your nose. In fact,
they are so obvious that you have walked right by them numerous times, discounting their importance. A clue is not
big and noisy; it does not jump up and down saying, "Pick
me! Pick me!" The clues to solving the riddle of who you
really are reside in the quiet space of joy.

---

### EXERCISE 12.2: FINDING CLUES
### TO YOUR UNIQUENESS

1. Sit in meditation, with your eyes closed and feet flat
   on the floor. Be in the center of your head, all alone.
   See your grounding cord fastened securely to the
   center of the earth, and see your aura clean and clear,
   filled with your own pristine energy.

2. Breathe and just be for a moment. Listen to the stillness. Validate that you have come a long way on this journey of discovery. Feel yourself surrounded by waves of energy that vibrate with your highest and best interest.

3. Check in with your earth and cosmic energies. Feel the earth energy coming up from the soles of your feet, up your legs, into your first chakra, and falling like water out the back of your first chakra. Feel the cosmic energy coming in at the top of your head and coursing down your back and into your first chakra. Now imagine the two energies merging and running up the front of your body, up through your torso, then your face, and finally shooting out the top of your head. See some of the mixture branching off at your throat, running down your arms, and spouting out of your palms.

4. As you sit in this meditative place, say your statement of being aloud. As you do so, ask that thoughts and words come to you about what joy means to you.

5. See images form in front of you; hear words whispered in your ears. Listen. See images of what joy is like for you.

6. Come out of meditation and write down the words, or draw the picture of joy.

Your Spirit, your Highest and Best Self, is always next to you, ready to guide you in the direction best suited for living your life on purpose. Sit in silence for a moment and review the words and images that bring you joy. Sit and feel. Sit and absorb. That is all.

Joy has many forms. Some people will immediately sense a direction and develop a plan of action to live in joy. Others will follow a less defined route. All is good. Spirit is here for each of us if we tune in and listen.

Read your statement of being aloud again as you remember the images of joy from the meditation. Write down some of the most descriptive words. Now think of what you are doing or being when time ceases to exist.

The answer to this question can come in many forms. You may be digging in the earth, tending your garden. Or you may be sitting at your desk, solving a huge accounting problem. You might be teaching or caring for a dear friend. It could very well be that your current job is not a source of joy, but it might be a way for you to pay for the dance class that does bring you joy. Spend a moment thinking of those times when you are not defined by time and space.

If you are a gardener, your life's purpose may entail being aware of Mother Earth and tending to her needs. Maybe joy takes the form of growing vegetables to share with your family and friends, volunteering at a community garden, or taking an active part in developing legislation to protect the local environment. Each of these is a possible path to your life's purpose. The importance lies in the be-ing, not the do-ing—being in joy, radiating joy through your thoughts and feelings.

If, in solving an accounting problem, the world ceases to exist and time stands still, then your analytical skills may give you a clue to your passion. Maybe you choose to express your joy by creating an intricate metal sculpture for a friend or designing and building a custom home for your family. Remember that the being is the important part of the equation; you are being on purpose when you exist in joy.

Your life's purpose may not be tied to how you earn an income. For me, this was a huge breakthrough. I spent years trying to come up with an occupation that gave me ecstatic joy. I had heard the phrase "Do what you love and the money will follow." That is definitely true for those people who know how to build a career around their passion. However, my jobs, which I truly valued, did not seem to fit the pattern. I realized that purpose is not necessarily tied to a paying position. Maybe your passion lies somewhere off the beaten path, as mine does.

Think about what brings you joy. Be in thought for a moment more. Just breathe and be. Bring to the surface of your memory times when you felt intense joy. Think of what you were doing when time stood still. Maybe you were surrounded by friends and family, or maybe you were alone. Write about it. Journal your memories of the times when you felt immense joy. We will work with this information very soon.

Often we become stuck trying to figure out what gives us joy. We know it when we experience it, but we can't quite figure out how to live like that all the time. Let's ask our younger self to give us some clues.

## EXERCISE 12.3: LEARNING JOY
## FROM THE CHILD YOU WERE

1. Sit in meditation and think about your life when you were a small child.

2. Have your eyes closed and your feet flat on the floor. Be in the center of your head, with your grounding cord around your hips. Run some earth and cosmic energies, and watch as the mixture streams through your body and out the top of your head and the palms of your hands. Sit and just breathe for a moment.

3. Now visualize a seven-year-old child in front of you. Recognize that this is you at the age of seven. Breathe the air of being seven. Remember that time. See that seven-year-old child standing in front of you.

4. Ask this seven-year-old to tell you about joy. Listen and watch as the child shows you what joy meant to you at that age. Even if life was rough at the age of seven, there were moments of joy mixed in among the pain. While you acknowledge that the pain exists, ask the child to show you the moments of joy.

5. Continue to watch as this child experiences the joys of life. Once the child has finished showing you what joy was like for you at seven, thank the child and watch them leave. Sit in meditation for a moment longer and feel those feelings. Just breathe.

6. When you are ready, open your eyes and begin to write or draw about what you just experienced.

Write down the feelings associated with the experience of joy. Words such as "wonder," "heart bursting open with happiness," "freedom," and "expansiveness" may come to mind. Remember the activities that brought you joy at a young age. Maybe you loved flying kites on a windy day or running up a hill and then rolling down. You're an adult now, and you may no longer relish water balloon fights, but the seven-year-old wants you to remember the feelings associated with play. Those "joy" words are important clues to living your life on purpose. Write down the words that resonate with you.

## Fitting the Pieces Together

The answer to this puzzle of how to live a life full of purpose and meaning is inside of you. It is now time to retrieve clues in order to answer the question "What is my purpose?" You have already removed the negative words and phrases that served as camouflage and hid the real you. Now go back through your work and remember the positives. The following exercise will help you synthesize all of this.

---

### EXERCISE 12.4: REVIEW YOUR JOURNEY

1. First, let's return to your original name web. Review it with the intent of pulling out the positive phrases representing your name. Write them down.

2. Now move on to your statement of being, circling the adjectives that best describe you.

3. Review your tree of life and the choices that bring you joy.

4. Review your notes from the chapters on relationships. Reflect upon the mirrors in your life and what lessons you are here to learn.

5. Check out the one million dollar test in chapter 9 for clues as to how you would live your life if you had all the money in the world.

6. Review the previous meditations in this chapter on joy. Think about how your seven-year-old self expressed joy.

7. What brings *you* joy?

To illustrate how this exercise can take hold in your life, I'll share two stories of people who came to a better understanding of what their life purpose truly is. The first story is about Amy, a self-employed business consultant. Amy's epiphany came as she saw her seven-year-old self standing in front of a case full of wooden puzzles. She remembered a teacher calling her a puzzle whiz, and she recalled the joy of completing a task that others couldn't. Amy saw the tie-in to her human resources career being the problem solver, the person others looked to when the challenges seemed insurmountable—that was her joy. Her major life lesson came into focus through the lens of a former boss who did not want an agent of change in the company. In the relationship chapter, Amy realized that her boss had been a major mirror for her. As they butted heads over changes in policy that would shake up the company, Amy's attitude had turned sour the moment her boss decided not to implement her recommendations. Amy's negative reaction to this defeat led to her ultimately being fired.

As she sat in meditation, Amy realized that her over-the-top reaction to the situation with her boss offered clues to an underlying life challenge. She remembered other times of feeling personally affronted and emotionally drained when her ideas were disregarded. By reviewing her name web and some of the most insidious phrases of her inner critic, Amy realized that her self-worth needed to be uncoupled from the acceptance of her recommendations. This was her aha moment. She knew her life purpose was still to be a catalyst, an agent of change, but she also knew now not to take it as a personal insult if her ideas were not acted upon. She realized that being her authentic self meant looking within for validation instead of attaching her self-worth to the ideas she put forth.

Amy is currently self-employed as a turn-around specialist for large corporations. She still expresses her joy in solving the puzzles of life, but from a different mindset. As she watches her ideas take root and move her client companies in new directions, she is mindful of affirming her own internal self-worth regardless of outcome. She has also started a practice of writing each client recommendation from the space of pure giving, without any expectation of return. She's found peace and is comfortable in her own skin, and that gives her joy.

In the middle of taking the one million dollar test, Calvin, a high school math teacher, realized that if he had all the money in the world, he would start a foundation to provide a free breakfast for anyone in need. This dream related directly to a memory from when he was seven and he gave away his school lunch to a very hungry friend. The exercise and subsequent memory also reinforced the positive name-web statements that Calvin had written: "caring," "nurturing," and "empathy." After much pondering, he realized that living his life on purpose meant giving to others with an open heart and in a state of gratitude. While he maintained his teaching job to pay the bills, Calvin spent his weekends volunteering at the local food bank. That was his joy, his purpose, his gift to the world.

Write about what brings you joy. Keep the thoughts fresh in your mind as you move on to the final exercise, which will help you bring your vision to life. To help put all the pieces together, I use a technique I call "treasure mapping," the process of assembling visual images and words that express living your life as you were meant to. Treasure mapping is a graphic representation of the images you saw and felt in the preceding meditation. This type of collage can also be referred to as a vision board, story board, or dream board.

Regardless of what you call it, a treasure map is an actual physical picture of your desired reality, calling like-minded energies into your reality. It helps you remember the various aspects of what joy means to you. Your desires for what you want to have, do, or be in your life come alive once they are in a visual format. Living a life on purpose means living a life full of joy and love. This treasure map will act as a visual reminder of your journey of discovery.

A treasure map is also a great manifesting tool because it forms an especially clear, sharp image to use as a basis for future mock-ups. It is now time to open up those manila envelopes you started in Exercise 4.3: Picturing Your Dream Life to see the photos that you have been looking at and collecting throughout your journey. Open the envelopes representing the adjectives that describe your feeling states and your statement of being words. You might have an envelope full of images representing kindness or peace or enthusiasm. Spill out the contents of those envelopes on the table in front of you. You might have images representing your feeling state of caring for others mixed in with images representing your feeling state of play or loyalty.

Now look at the images. Really look. Spend some time reviewing the images as you remember why you chose to cut out that picture or draw that particular scene.

Place similar-themed pictures together. Maybe you are surprised to find that most of your pictures are of people laughing together over coffee, or of being active in some way. Or perhaps your images show more solitary pursuits, such as studying, reading, or writing. Cluster together images that are all about family or activities done in a group. See what general theme comes to mind. Close your eyes and allow yourself a moment to dream. Ask for Spirit to guide you to your life purpose.

In the next exercise, you will make a collage, a visual representation, to remind you of what joy means to you and how to live a life full of purpose and meaning.

---

### EXERCISE 12.5: A TREASURE MAP OF JOY

1. In creating your treasure map, look for convenient and exciting ways to visually display your work. You may use a piece of poster board or any large piece of paper, such as from an artist's sketchpad. Or you may

decide that a piece of corkboard allows you to change out your display as your creativity expands and your specific mock-ups come into reality. Anything goes in treasure mapping, so use your imagination and allow Spirit to act as your guide.

2. You'll need scissors and glue sticks or some other type of adhesive. You will also need colored pencils, markers, pens, and crayons. You might want to add some glitter and whimsy representing the cosmos and Spirit.

3. Write out your statement of being and give it a prominent place on your map. Add whatever visuals you would like in order to make your statement stand out. Add your heart traits and any information from your name web or money web that feels appropriate.

4. Include a picture of yourself on your treasure map, along with a symbol of the Divine that has meaning and power for you. It could be rays of golden sun energy permeating your images, or a powerful representation of your Spirit.

5. This map is all about joy and life purpose, so be sure to include some images representing the feeling states of joy. Excitement, exuberance, enthusiasm, tranquility, peace, grace, acceptance of All That Is: these all could be among the feeling states that express joy for you.

6. Allow Spirit to guide you as you let your creativity flow. Anything goes. Spend some time creating your map of life purpose.

7. Once you feel complete, display your work where you will see it every day. Ask that inspiration come to you about multiple ways to live your life *on purpose*.

I hope you have learned to validate the wonderfully exquisite being that you are. Living a life on purpose means that you are filled with joy and enthusiasm. You know your life's purpose deep within your core, and you gladly share this gift with others. We are all connected. As you raise your frequency to match your unique purpose, you raise the vibration of the thoughts and feelings you transmit into the world. Think of that. As you think and feel joy and love and enthusiasm, those thought forms travel from you to others around you. As other people pick up those vibrations, they will begin to match that higher vibration. Like attracts like. Your thoughts are beacons of knowingness, calling back to you events and circumstances that allow you to shine bright and stand tall.

That is grace.

Following your purpose in the deepest sense means that you are not concerned with the shoulds of the world. It is not about what you do that is important, it is about the *attitude and feelings you bring to what you do.* When your thoughts, feelings, beliefs, words, and actions support your life's purpose, you are in grace. That is the joy. As you come to know, deep within your soul, that you are living a life full of inner purpose and meaning, you radiate this joy out into the world, affecting everyone around you.

You are here on Earth to discover your Higher Self, your Spirit, and to listen to your own internal wisdom. As you do this, you understand that your true mission in life is to express your unique gift—and to share it with the world.

Let's do one last meditation together.

---

### EXERCISE 12.6: FINDING YOUR UNIQUE GIFT

1. Sit in silence. Be in the center of your head. See your grounding cord around your hips, stretching down to the center of the earth. See your aura fused to your grounding cord, offering an airtight seal. Ask that your grounding cord be on maximum release. See foreign energy leave your space and siphon down to the center of the earth. Be in stillness. Breathe. See your aura bubble in a protective coating of your choice. Intend for any foreign energy to be deflected before it can enter your space. Feel alone, at peace, centered, and still.

2. Now visualize a bubble of energy in front of you. Intend for that bubble to represent your original essence, that beam of light, your soul essence. See that bubble grow bigger and brighter in front of you. See it full of colors that especially represent you: just you, your uniqueness, your specialness. No one else on this planet is exactly like you. Marvel at the colors; see the exquisite details of the swirls and waves of color. This is *you*. This is your shining light. Say hello to this energy and receive a hello back. Maybe you see the colors representing kindness, gentleness, or wisdom. Or you might sense the energies of playfulness, enthusiasm, or humor.

3. Now ask for words to form in your mind—words that let you know who you really are. See phrases form, and see pictures develop in front of you. This is your Spirit speaking to you. Sit. Breathe. Listen. Watch.

4. Once the bubble is full of the energy of your soul, of your uniqueness, then grab that bubble and pull it right into your aura. Infuse your space with the colors and feelings of your Spirit, your true essence. Maybe you see colors of gold, light blue, lavender, and pink swirling around in your aura. Maybe you feel the energies of love, peace, compassion, understanding, respect, and self-worth throughout your body.

5. Ask that a special, smaller ball of this energy form in the center of your heart space. Ask for this special ball of vibrating colors and feelings to infuse you with the sense of your own self-worth. Feel your own essence, your own specialness, shining forth from your heart space. See beacons of this light emanate from you in all directions. See these waves of oscillating energies penetrating far and wide. You are a powerful beacon, sending light into the world and sharing your gift with all. Intend for these rays of energy to continue to shine, even after this meditation is complete.

6. When you feel complete, open your eyes and come out of meditation. Know that your aura is infused with the color of *you* and that the rays of your essence continue to shine forth.

As you come out of meditation, spend a moment sitting in stillness. What is your unique gift to the world, and how might you share this gift? Write or draw whatever thoughts come to mind. Give yourself plenty of time, and if you want to return to the meditation to gather more information, then do so.

Living a life on purpose is living a life in joy. It is knowing, deep down in the seat of your soul, what brings you joy. As you focus on that which brings you joy—and as you allow yourself to express this joy through your job, your family, and your relationships—you will attract more and more events and circumstances that are in alignment with your purpose. That is the miracle. That is grace.

Namasté. I see you. Go in peace.

# Resources and Suggestions for Further Study

If you have enjoyed our work together and would like to continue into a deeper and more profound acceptance of yourself and others, then I suggest looking into the following programs and books. First and foremost:

### *Boulder Psychic Institute in Boulder, Colorado:*
### *http://boulderpsychicinstitute.org*

Choose your thoughts. Choose your emotions. Choose your life. Boulder Psychic Institute is a spiritual sanctuary for individuals seeking truth, freedom, and peace in this lifetime. Director and founder Miwa Mack teaches students to open up to their own psychic abilities in an atmosphere of ease, fun, and nonjudgment. There is nothing "woo-woo" about this program. It is a down-to-earth, easy-to-understand guide to opening up your own psychic abilities. I am a graduate of this program, and under Miwa's guidance and tutelage I have tamed my inner critic and I am living my life on purpose. I shine bright because of the work I have done here. Thanks,

Miwa! Tele-classes allow students from all over the world to participate.

### Psychic Horizons Center in Boulder, Colorado: www.psychichorizonscenter.org

Co-founder and co-director Mary Bell Nyman and co-director Hope Hewetson have said that people attracted to classes at Psychic Horizons Center know that energy is real, and they want to learn to work with it. Students learn to access their inner wisdom and use it to create their own reality by taking charge of their experiences. I have studied at Psychic Horizons as well, and I have found this program to be full of fun, playfulness, and awareness. As Mary Bell says, "Energy is not fussy." Learn to open to your clairvoyance from a space of fun and ease.

## Books to Speed You on Your Journey of Discovery

*The Subtle Body: An Encyclopedia of Your Energetic Anatomy* by Cyndi Dale (Sounds True, 2009). A comprehensive, fully illustrated reference book of the human energy system. I was astounded at the information housed in this one volume. A must-read for anyone interested in the world of energy awareness.

*You Are Psychic: The Art of Clairvoyant Reading & Healing* by Debra Lynne Katz (Llewellyn Publications, 2004). This practical guide is easy to follow and perfect for anyone interested in developing or strengthening their psychic abilities.

*The Energy of Money: A Spiritual Guide to Financial and Personal Fulfillment* by Maria Nemeth, PhD (Ballantine Publishing Group, 1997). Dr. Nemeth explores the tool called money and how to harness its energy to fulfill your life's dreams. Full of exercises and how-tos.

*The Soul of Money: Transforming Your Relationship with Money and Life* by Lynne Twist (W. W. Norton & Company, 2003). Ms. Twist delves into the soulful purpose that money can play in your life and how prosperity and abundance are represented by more than just our material possessions.

*Your Soul's Plan: Discovering the Real Meaning of the Life You Planned Before You Were Born* by Robert Schwartz (Frog Books, 2007). If you are skeptical about but interested in reincarnation, this is a great place to start. Through case studies, Mr. Schwartz follows four trance mediums as they work with clients to uncover the reasons they face their particular life challenges.

*The Not So Big Life: Making Room for What Really Matters* by Sarah Susanka (Random House, 2007). If you are ready to declutter and move to a more simple way of living, you will enjoy Ms. Susanka's exercises designed to help you remodel your life to fit who you are right now.

*Energy Medicine: Balancing Your Body's Energies for Optimal Health, Joy, and Vitality* by Donna Eden, with David Feinstein, PhD (Jeremy P. Tarcher, 1998). This easy-to-follow, illustrated guide to energy medicine is another must-have book.

## More Recommended Reading

*A Life of Being, Having, and Doing Enough* by Wayne Muller (Random House, 2010).

*Conversations with God: An Uncommon Dialogue, Books 1, 2, and 3* by Neale Donald Walsch (G. P. Putnam's Sons, 1996).

*Getting into the Vortex: Guided Meditations Audio and User Guide* by Esther and Jerry Hicks (Hay House, 2010). Based on the teachings of Abraham.

*Loving What Is: Four Questions That Can Change Your Life* by Byron Katie, with Stephen Mitchell (Three Rivers Press, 2002).

*Wherever You Go, There You Are: Mindfulness Meditation in Everyday Life* by Jon Kabat-Zinn (Hyperion, 1994). The quintessential guide to mindfulness.

EXPERIENCING PASSION & SERENITY THROUGH
BREATHWORK & MEDITATION

# RADICAL
## AWARENESS

# 5
## PRACTICES
### FOR A
## FULLY ENGAGED
## LIFE

# CATHERINE
# DOWLING

"*Radical Awareness* is a clear, useful handbook for dealing with some
of the basic issues in living a thoughtful life."
—THOMAS MOORE, *New York Times* bestseller author of *Care of the Soul*

# Radical Awareness
## *5 Practices for a Fully Engaged Life*
### CATHERINE DOWLING

Experience a profound engagement with life through the transformational power of spiritual awakenings. Presenting a simple and safe system that can be applied to daily living, *Radical Awareness* shows you how to achieve the mystical state of oneness. Join author Catherine Dowling as she offers meditation techniques, hands-on exercises, and breathwork methods for enlightenment and expanded awareness.

Exploring five practices for turning everyday experiences into opportunities for spiritual growth, you will learn to move past fear and self-sabotage, break the bonds of anger, understand the expectations of others, honor your own values, and more. Grounded in the knowledge of ancient and contemporary world wisdom traditions, *Radical Awareness* is a down-to-earth, workable guide for living with passion, abundance, and serenity.

**978-0-7387-4014-0, 288 pp., 6 x 9**                    **$16.99**

---

CYNDI DALE

*the*

# SPIRITUAL
# POWER

*of*

*empathy*

Develop Your Intuitive Gifts
for Compassionate Connection

# The Spiritual Power of Empathy
*Develop Your Intuitive Gifts for*
*Compassionate Connection*
CYNDI DALE

For some the empathic gift provides insight and inspiration, but for others empathy creates feelings of confusion and panic. *The Spiritual Power of Empathy* is a hands-on training course for empaths, showing you how to comfortably use this often-unrecognized ability for better relationships, career advancement, raising children, and healing the self and others.

Join popular author Cyndi Dale as she shares ways to develop the six empathic types, techniques for screening and filtering information, and tips for opening up to a new world of deeper connections with the loved ones in your life. Also includes important information for dealing with the difficulties empaths often face, such as being overwhelmed in a crowd.

**978-0-7387-3799-7, 264 pp., 6 x 9**                    **$16.99**

---

# Psychic Abilities

# For Beginners

Awaken Your Intuitive Senses

Melanie Barnum

# Psychic Abilities for Beginners
## *Awaken Your Intuitive Senses*
### Melanie Barnum

There's more to this lifetime than the naked eye can see, and *Psychic Abilities for Beginners* is the perfect guide to this unseen knowledge. When you develop your psychic skills, you will increase your confidence, stimulate your potential, and expose the magnificence that is already inside you. With true stories of actual psychic events and tips and techniques for starting your intuitive journey, author Melanie Barnum will help you:

- Discover your psychic senses with hands-on exercises
- Identify your unique psychic strengths
- Use your intuitive abilities to manifest abundance
- Enhance your relationships, career, and financial situation
- Overcome challenges and create a life you'll love

**978-0-7387-4028-7, 336 pp., 5³⁄₁₆ x 8          $15.99**

Melissa Alvarez

# 365 WAYS

## to RAISE Your

## FREQUENCY

SIMPLE TOOLS TO INCREASE
YOUR SPIRITUAL ENERGY
FOR BALANCE, PURPOSE, AND JOY

# 365 Ways to Raise Your Frequency
*Simple Tools to Increase Your Spiritual Energy*
*for Balance, Purpose, and Joy*

MELISSA ALVAREZ

The soul's vibrational rate, our spiritual frequency, has a huge impact on our lives. As it increases, so does our capacity to calm the mind, connect with angels and spirit guides, find joy and enlightenment, and achieve what we want in life.

This simple and inspiring guide makes it easy to elevate your spiritual frequency every day. Choose from a variety of ordinary activities, such as singing and cooking. Practice visualization exercises and techniques for reducing negativity, manifesting abundance, tapping into Universal Energy, and connecting with your higher self. Discover how generous actions and a positive attitude can make a difference. You'll also find long-term projects and guidance for boosting your spiritual energy to new heights over a lifetime.

**978-0-7387-2740-0, 432 pp., 5 x 7**           **$16.95**

---

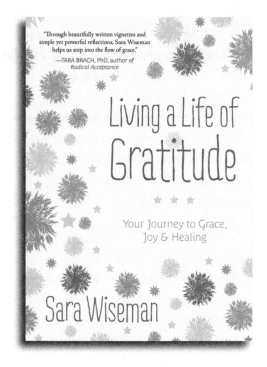

"Through beautifully written vignettes and simple yet powerful reflections, Sara Wiseman helps us step into the flow of grace."
—TARA BRACH, PhD, author of *Radical Acceptance*

# Living a Life of
# Gratitude

★ ★ ★

Your Journey to Grace,
Joy & Healing

Sara Wiseman

# Living a Life of Gratitude
## *Your Journey to Grace, Joy & Healing*
### Sara Wiseman

When you walk through life with gratitude and simply appreciating everything, every single thing, you reconnect with what's truly important in life. The awe and wonder of life is now ever present.

Through 88 illuminating short stories, *Living a Life of Gratitude* will help you slow down, look around, and see your life for what it is. From our first breaths to our last, Sara Wiseman explores the landmarks of human experience: that we are able to be children and have children, that we can learn and love! Even if we have little, we have so much. Read this book, and revel in the beauty of the world.

**978-0-7387-3753-9, 384 pp., 5 x 7** **$16.99**

---

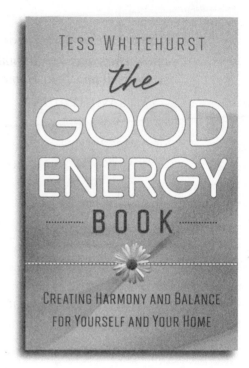

TESS WHITEHURST

*the*

# GOOD
# ENERGY
## BOOK

CREATING HARMONY AND BALANCE
FOR YOURSELF AND YOUR HOME